AWAKEN, CHILDREN!

Dialogues With
Sri Mata Amritanandamayi

VOLUME 6

Adaptation & Translation

SWAMI AMRITASWARUPANANDA

Mata Amritanandamayi Center, San Ramon
California, United States

AWAKEN, CHILDREN!
Volume 6

Published by:
  Mata Amritanandamayi Center
  P.O. Box 613
  San Ramon, CA 94583
  United States

In India:
  www.amritapuri.org
  inform@amritapuri.org

In Europe:
  www.amma-europe.org

In US:
  www.amma.org

This Book is Humbly Offered at the
LOTUS FEET OF HER HOLINESS
SRI MATA AMRITANANDAMAYI
The Resplendent Luminary Immanent
In the Hearts of All Beings

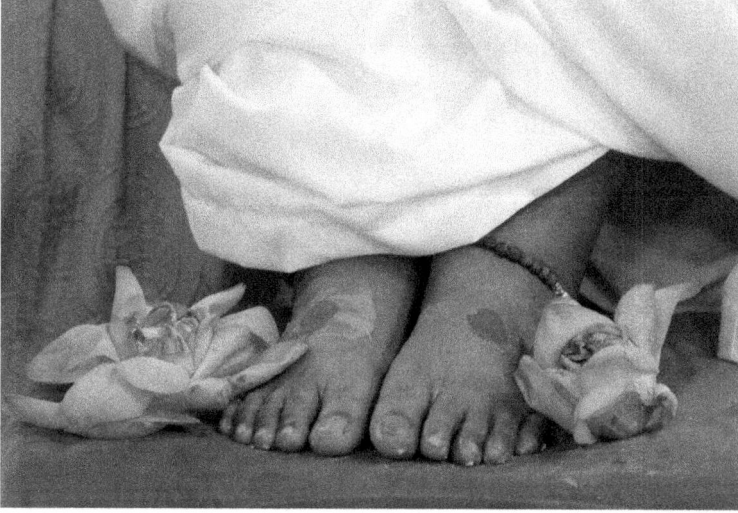

Vandeham saccidānandam bhāvātītam jagatgurum |
Nityam pūrnam nirākāram nirgunam svātmasamsthitam | |
I prostrate to the Universal Teacher, Who is Satchidananda (Pure
Being-Knowledge-Absolute Bliss), Who is beyond all differences,
Who is eternal, all-full, attributeless, formless and ever-centered
in the Self.

Saptasāgaraparyantam tīrthasnānaphalam tu yat |
Gurupādapayōvindōh sahasrāmsena tatphalam | |
Whatever merit is acquired by one, through pilgrimmages and
from bathing in the Sacred Waters extending to the seven seas,
cannot be equal to even one thousandth part of the merit derived
from partaking the water with which the Guru's Feet are washed.

Guru Gita, verses 157, 87

Contents

Chapter 1

The Amritapuri Ashram lies on a narrow peninsula off the southwest coast of India. Bordered by the Arabian Sea on one side, and Kerala's famous backwaters on the other, Mother's Ashram has today become popular even among those who pass by on the daily backwaters tours. When it was first registered in 1981, the Ashram consisted of just the small plot of land which was Mother's family's property. Where the colorful temple now towers above the coconut palms, and hundreds of devotees and disciples live permanently, there was only a handful of residents living in a group of huts near the small temple that still stands today. In those days the residents enjoyed very few luxuries or amenities, but no one seemed to mind; the loving presence of the Divine Mother created a safe and solid haven.

A great healer of hearts

Monday, 16 July, 1984

A man who was mentally ill came to the Ashram, escorted by his family. He was screaming and shouting as he arrived. He cried and then he laughed. One moment he made strange, contradictory statements, the next moment he cried aloud, running about erratically. His wife and older brother followed him at all times, watching carefully that he came to no harm. It was obvious that the man was experiencing deep mental agony and pain. His family cried, helpless to ease the pathetic condition of their loved one. Before coming to see Mother, the family had tried several medical treatments, but the young man's condition persisted. Having heard about Mother from a distant relative, they decided to come and see Her with the hope that She could help their son. This was their first visit to the Ashram.

The entire family waited for Mother at the bottom of the staircase leading to Her room. Because She was expected soon, they held on tightly to the sick man to prevent him from running away. He kept on laughing, crying and muttering to himself. At last Mother came down. Bursting into tears, the man's mother and his young wife fell at Mother's feet, and begged Her through their tears to relieve him from his pain. The father explained his son's story to Mother. The young man had lost a great deal of money in a business deal with some unscrupulous people. He had trusted them, and the shock of such a great loss was more than he could bear.

Though his family cried in Mother's presence, the young man was still. At one point he said to Mother quite calmly, "You know, Amma, I lost everything. Can you help me? Can you save me?" Then he began to sob.

As She observed his pitiful state and listened to the man's heart-rending words, Mother's eyes filled with tears. She consoled each member of the family, expressing immense love and compassion for them. Turning towards the mentally ill man, She rubbed his forehead and chest with the love and care that a mother would show her own child. Placing his head on Her shoulder, Mother said, "Son, don't worry. Relax. Everything will be all right. Be patient." For some time Mother continued to rub his back and to soothe him with Her gentle words.

Mother spent a few more minutes with the family before moving towards the *darshan* hut. She had not given them any specific instructions or advice, and as they were left standing at the bottom of the staircase, they felt a bit confused. Their confusion soon vanished however, for, just before entering the hut, Mother turned around. "Children," She said, "wait till darshan has finished. Amma will see you again then."

While the darshan was in progress, the family waited outside. During the entire darshan the sick man remained sitting near the hut, in a surprisingly calm mood. His family was very happy to see this change.

As soon as Mother came out of the darshan hut, She went straight to the sick man, took him by the hand, and led him to the northern side of the Ashram. It was a charming sight to see him walking behind Her like a small child dutifully following his mother. At one point he released his grip from Mother's hand and tried to run away. In no time Mother coaxed him back to Her. When they reached a water tap, Mother sent someone to fetch a bucket and a mug and asked the young man to sit down. Though at first he would not obey, once again, through Her compassionate words and loving caresses, Mother reassured the man, and he finally sat down under the tap. As soon as She turned the tap on, however, the man jumped up and once again tried to run away, but this time Mother held him firmly by the shoulder and said, "No, my son, no. Sit down. Calm down. Don't run away. This is for your own good. It will make you better. Don't you want to feel better? Don't you want to be healthy again? You want to work and look after your family, don't you? Sit quietly." Mother's words seemed to have a soothing effect on the man, and he again became calm.

By this time someone had arrived with a bucket and a mug. Mother filled the bucket and began pouring the water over the man's head. A beaming smile spread across Her face and, clearly delighted, She continued to pour water over him for a long time.

Finally Mother turned off the tap saying, "That is enough." Yet the man remained seated. "Son, you can get up now," Mother said. He immediately got up. Someone handed Her a towel, and Mother wiped his face, chest and back. Turning to his family who had stood by observing the whole scene, Mother said, "Change his dhoti, but don't dry his hair. Let it dry by itself."

The parents of the sick man had not looked away even for a moment while Mother was with their son. They were obviously deeply moved by the way Mother cared for him, by how She had bathed him, all the while showering him with boundless love. Now, as Her attention shifted to them, they started to cry; they had been holding back their tears for a long time. Taking them in Her arms, and placing their heads on Her shoulders, Mother embraced each of them and wiped away their tears.

By now, Mother's clothes were also wet. One of the *brahmacharis* pointed this out to Her. "That's okay," She replied. "There was a time when Mother's clothes were always wet from carrying water and rice gruel for the cows, from wading through the backwaters looking for the ducks, and from constantly being engaged in household chores. Amma used to remain in the backwaters and in the rain for hours on end. She is used to it. It is not a problem now."

Mother stayed with the family for a few more minutes and left only after instructing them to stay in the Ashram for a few days. On the second day, Mother again bathed the man; this time he remained quiet and calm. Already there was a big change in him.

Whilethis incident is an outstanding example of Mother's humility and love, there are countless similar incidents which exemplify Her infinite love, compassion and patience. In the late 1970's, many mentally ill people came to stay near Her. Mother used to take care of them, bathing them, feeding them, and looking after them as if they were Her own children. Back then, however, Mother's compassionate ways did not always appeal to Her family members. Their property was very small, occupying only a tenth of an acre of land. Aside from the main house, a cow shed, and a small temple, there was no shelter from the rain and sun. The property was also surrounded by water, making it a hazardous playground for these disturbed people, who were in the habit of screaming, shouting and running about. Sometimes they even tried to attack Mother.

While Mother patiently endured everything and continued to serve these people with patience and love, eventually Her father and older brother summoned their relatives and ordered them to take them back home. Not only was their presence disruptive, but they simply could not be accommodated in a safe and suitable way. Although sorry to see them go, Mother did not object to their leaving, for She was well aware of the lack of facilities for them and of the hardships they caused Her family.

Though these people were not able to stay permanently with Mother, certainly the contact they had with Her, intimate as it was, had a profound effect. Being fed, bathed and cared for by Mother as if She were their mother, these mentally ill people made great progress under Mother's loving and powerful care.

Countless people have experienced miraculous recoveries through Mother's Grace, but one especially memorable case is that of a leper namedDattan. He used to come for the *Devi Bhava* darshan every Tuesday, Thursday,and Sunday. On these three nights, Mother had a regular routine. Just before entering the temple, She would dance in ecstasy, holding a sword in one hand and a trident in the other. Moving around the temple, She would sometimes stop Her dance in order to bless people with a touch of Her sword. Dattan stood at a certain spot just behind the temple, ready with a few pitchers of water and a towel around his waist. Mother always paused from Her dance to pour each pitcher of water over the leper's head. She bathed him in this way three times a week, until he was cured of his disease.

Mother's life has always been one of sacrifice, with every moment devoted to alleviating the suffering of others.

. She Herself says, "It is Amma's sincere wish that Her hands will be caressing and consoling a distressed person at the very moment She breathes Her last breath, even when She has little energy left in Her body." Mother's tireless actions and continuous compassion in every moment of Her life show the true meaning of Her words.

The sick man got better. After some months, he and his entire family returned to the Ashram. They said that all the symptoms of the mental disease had slowly disappeared after they had returned home. During the few days they had stayed at the Ashram, Mother had instructed the man to discontinue all medication.

Convinced that the young man's recovery was the gift of Mother's Grace, the whole family was overwhelmed with gratitude and joy. Once his sickness was cured, he was able to get back all the money he had lost, and with it start a business on his own. Responding to their heartfelt words of thanks, Mother smilingly said, "Children, now that you are happy do not forget God. Remember Him and pray to Him even in times of happiness. Usually people remember God and pray to Him only when they are in pain, as if God were only a pain-destroyer. Don't be like that. Let prayer and remembrance of God become part of your daily life. Amma is always with you."

That night everyone gathered in front of the temple for the evening *bhajan*. Mother sang the lead as everybody sang the response to

Devi saranam

Give me refuge, O Goddess,
Give me refuge.
O Mother, whose divine form is being praised
By the celestial beings,
O Primal, Supreme Energy,
Salutations to You!

O Giver of auspiciousness,
The Universe exists within You;
Everything is born out of You,
And it is known that everything
Eventually dissolves into You alone.

O Mother,
As I prostrate at Your Feet,
Let me pray with all my devotion,
For just one thing;
I pray that Your pure, effulgent Form
Will shine in me forever
And that my tongue
Will constantly enjoy the taste
Of repeating Your Name.

The millions of living beings
Are all parts of the one Whole;
They are like waves of the Ocean.
This Universe has been designed
To help all beings attain their Liberation.

When we come to know
That our very life is nothing but You,
We become detached from this world

Like an actor who takes off his costume
At the end of a good performance.

After the evening bhajan, Mother continued to sit on the front verandah of the temple. The singing had transported everyone to another plane, and all were filled with love and devotion. Some residents meditated, while others sat gazing at Mother, who was leaning against the wall, lost to this world. After some time, Mother moved and lay down on the bare floor. Like iron filings shifting with the slightest movement of a powerful magnet, everybody gathered closer to Her. As She lay there, Mother raised both hands up and called out, "Shivane!" The next moment everybody heard Mother say to Herself, "He cannot hear you. Such a mindless fellow. He is a mindless fellow."

The next moment Mother sat up and sang

Shiva Shiva Hara Hara

O Auspicious One,
Destroyer of that which is unreal,
Who is clothed in the clouds,
O Beautiful One,
Who is playing the damaru drum.

Who holds the trident in His hand,
Bestowing fearlessness and boons,
Who has locks of matted hair
And limbs covered with ashes.

Who is adorned with a garland of cobras
And a necklace of human skulls,
Who supports the crescent moon on His forehead
And whose eyes are full of compassion.

O Auspicious One,
O Destroyer,
Great God.

The devotees responded with enthusiasm to this lively song. It sounded as if a second session of evening bhajans had begun. The singing went on for some time, and when it ended, Mother returned to Her normal mood.

One of the devotees began to talk about his granddaughter who was barely four years old. Pointing to the child, the man said, "Amma, this girl really loves you. She expresses great devotion for you. Sometimes She covers her head with a piece of white cloth, enters the *puja* room, and sings bhajans, swaying back and forth and sideways just like you. After the bhajan she calls everybody and distributes sacred ash, saying that she is Vallikkavilamma. What a girl she is!"

Mother called the little girl to Her and asked, "Dear child, when you grow up will you have as much *bhakti* as you have now? Will you be as innocent then?"

The child nodded her head. Obviously proud of the girl, her grandfather became excited and said, "Daughter, tell Ammachi who your mother is." Without any hesitation, the little girl answered, "My mother is not Girijamma (her biological mother). Vallikkavilamma is my mother."

"Child, why do you love Amma?" Mother asked.

The little girl's reply was immediate, "Because Amma is God."

Upon hearing this, Mother was delighted. She laughed aloud and embraced the child, rocking her in Her arms. Mother then sat the girl on Her lap and playfully pleaded with her to sing a bhajan. In a hesitant voice, the girl sang the first four lines of

Kamesha vamakshi

Salutations to Shakti, the Great Goddess,
Who is accessible through devotion;
Salutations to the Seed, the One Truth,
Infinite and Perfect Awareness.

Mother was so pleased with her that She kissed the child on both cheeks. She rocked the little girl back and forth, and they both smiled and laughed with glee. This playful excitement gradually subsided and soon, the meowing of a cat was heard in the dark. "Here Chakki, here Chakki." Mother called out, looking in the direction of the meowing. Mother continued to call, "Here, Chakki. Where are you? Come here."

Within a few seconds the cat jumped onto the verandah from the side of the temple. It came straight up to Mother and started rubbing its body against Her arm. Next, it jumped right into Mother's lap, trying to find a way to curl up comfortably. Since the little girl was still sitting on Mother's lap, the cat's attempts to settle there made everybody laugh. Mother remarked, "Chakki is very jealous." Again laughter filled the air.

One brahmachari excitedly said, "Amma, if animals feel jealous, why should it be surprising if we too feel that way? When even animals love to be on Your lap, you shouldn't deny us that pleasure." Again there was laughter.

The art of dying

The atmosphere grew more serious when one of the brahmacharis asked a question, "Amma, we have heard you say repeatedly that the *Mahatmas* (Great Souls) and the scriptures all state that one should have the urgency to realize the Self, or to break the shackles of worldly bondage. What do you mean by this urgency?"

Removing the girl from Her lap, Mother replied, "It is the urgency to know God, or the Self. Suppose you are diagnosed with a very serious illness. The doctors say you must immediately start taking such-and-such a medicine and not to delay. What will you do? You will try to get the medicine right away. You may find out that the medicine is very expensive, but that's all right. You don't care about the price. And if it is not available locally, you go to the next town. If it is not available there, you go to the nearest city. You may even have to go to another country to undergo treatment or surgery. So you do what is needed. You do not hesitate to take these steps. Of course, there are people who cannot afford to do this, but most people will do whatever they can to find a cure. Why? Because the disease is a threat to their life and they do not want to die. You do not want to leave this beautiful world and all that is precious to you. You do not want to leave the people and things that you love. The very thought of death makes you tremble.

"Just try to imagine how it will be when you die. The body that your dear ones, your wife, children, and parents have loved so much will be carried to the burial ground. No one wants to keep it. Nobody even wants to look at it. The very sight of it is frightening. Everybody wants to get rid of it as soon as possible. So your body will be taken to the graveyard. Or, someone will light the funeral pyre, and you are finished forever. The thought that after your death the world will continue without you makes you tremble. The world will go on without you, and you are going to miss everything that is beautiful: your house, your friends, your pretty young wife, your children, the flowers in the garden and their fragrance. The thought that you won't see any of them, that you won't see the cute, smiling face of your son again, the thought that you are going to miss all that you love makes you feel miserable. Nature and all its beauty, the rivers, the mountains and valleys, the sun and the moon, the stars, the ocean - no more will you see them. Festivals and celebrations, the loving and comforting words of your wife or husband, the affectionate caresses of your loved ones, everything will disappear. You don't know where you will go, but you presume that you will be surrounded by nothing but darkness. You are helpless. Can you imagine this? The very thought of death frightens you. Just imagining the helpless state you will be in when death comes can create an urgent desire to save your life. This urgency, then, is the intense longing to embrace the life-saving principle, the Supreme Truth. It is the longing to realize the immortality of the Self.

"Many people do not want to meditate because the stillness experienced in meditation makes them think that they are going to die. Sugunanandan Acchan (Amma's father) had great fear whenever Amma meditated. Amma was told that he thought She was going to die whenever Her meditation lasted for more than a few hours. In order to save Amma from dying, he would shake Her violently or pour buckets of water over Her head. Poor Acchan, he had no idea about meditation. He did not know that meditation is the saving principle, that it makes you immortal and eternal. Meditation takes you across the cycle of death and rebirth. Meditation is ambrosia. It actually prevents the fear of death. It makes you egoless, and takes you to the state of no-mind. Once you transcend the mind, you cannot die. Meditation and spiritual practices give you the power and courage to smile at death. Meditation helps you to see everything as a delightful play, so that even the moment of death becomes a blissful experience.

"So, children, this urgency comes when all your hopes and dreams collapse. They are bound to collapse because you are searching for happiness in the wrong place, where you cannot get it.

"A man was crawling around on his hands and knees. 'What are you searching for?' asked another person. 'My key.' Both men got on their knees to search. After a while the neighbor said, 'Where did you lose it?' 'At home.' 'Good Lord!' said the neighbor. 'Then why are you searching here?' 'Because it is brighter here.'

"Likewise, happiness is within you, but you search for it outside. For this reason, frustration is inevitable. You begin to feel that your life is in danger and that you cannot depend on anything but God or a Universal Power. The fear that death is going to take everything away from you makes you search for a way out. The search eventually takes you to the real path, the spiritual path. Your search for a way to conquer death will finally take you to your real Self.

"Man wants to live forever. No one wants to die. 'Life and love, not death' is the instinct that reverberates within every living being. Human beings want to live and live and live. They have an urge to cling to everything they possibly can, even the entire universe. They don't want to lose anything. There are such a variety of ways and techniques suggested by so many people around the world on how to live. They advertise, 'Gain your heart's desire in ten easy steps,' or any such slogan to tempt you to buy their method of gaining happiness and contentment. But what a pity! Nobody hits upon the real path except the true seeker. Nowhere in the world can one learn how to die; how to die to the ego, to attachments, anger, fear, and all that keeps you from attaining perfect peace. Man does not know that in the process of possessing, mastering and gaining, he is unconsciously losing. He is getting closer and closer to a great loss, a loss which he can never make up again. He will lose the chance of transcending the cycle of death and rebirth, which is the real purpose of this life in human form. The very thought, 'I am losing, not gaining at all,' can sometimes help you feel the urgency and come to the spiritual path."

Everybody sat in awe of Mother's words. She continued, "Children, you all know the great saint Tulsidas.[1] Of course we know him as a saint now, but before his spiritual quest he was a businessman. He was madly in love with his wife, and his attachment to her, his physical craving for her, was so intense that he did not even want to go to work. Once when she went to her parental home, Tulsidas's craving for her grew so uncontrollable that he walked a long distance in the dark, through wind and rain, just to be with her. So determined was he, that he mistook a dead body for a boat to cross a torrential river. Finally, after midnight, he reached his destination only to discover that all the doors were locked. Since his wife's room was on the upper floor, he had to climb in order to reach her room. Taking a python to be a thick rope, he scaled it and slipped into his wife's room. After all his difficulties, he expected his wife to be happy to see him. But instead, she was so ashamed of his insane attachment to her that she said to him, 'Had you directed this craving you have for me towards God, you would have realized God long ago.'

"Those words came as a shock to Tulsidas, a blow to his ego, and he himself must have felt extremely ashamed of his unintelligent and foolish attachment to her. He must have felt the burden of his attachment. Thus his whole being, every cell, every atom of his body, every heartbeat, every breath, and every pore of his body turned inward. That very moment he realized the heavy burden of attachment he had been carrying in the name of love. His heart skipped a beat to unload it and then was filled with pure love for God. At that moment he decided to die to his body-consciousness and to live in God-consciousness. He left his

---

[1] Tulsidas wrote Ramacharita Manas, another version of the Ramayana epic originally written by Valmiki.

wife and home and wandered as an ascetic. Later he became the renowned saint we know as Tulsidas."

After a few minutes Mother continued, "The moment of revelation that has occurred to many great souls can happen to you as well. Everybody is being prepared to reach this final state of dropping all worldly attachments, all ego. It must happen because that is the final stage of evolution. You cannot avoid it. Consciously or unconsciously, you may try to avoid it today, but sooner or later you are going to lose your grip on everything, possessions, wealth, body, all that you claim as your own. You think there is infinite time for you to live. But the awareness is growing each moment, even without your knowledge. The final destiny for all souls is the dropping away of every obstruction to peace and contentment. When that moment comes, the ego is dropped, and you won't struggle any more. You will neither protest, nor will you even pause to think whether you should let go or not. You will just bow down and surrender. Deep within, every soul is waiting for this great letting go to happen. Most people do not feel this now because their awareness is so low, but that urgency will come one day."

A *brahmachari* asked, "Amma, you said 'Nowhere in the world can one learn how to die.' Is death something that can be learned? Can you please explain?"

"Yes, death is an art to learn and practice. It can only be practiced if you drop your ego. It can only be learned by practicing meditation.

"Because death is the greatest threat, the greatest fear, the greatest blow to ourego, each moment human beings try to cover up and forget this fear of death by running after the pleasures of the world. In order to avert the thought of death people want to indulge themselves and enjoy life by creating and fulfilling desires.

"Children, with each birthday we take another step closer to death. It is also a 'deathday'. Birthdays come as a reminder of that fatal day, or the moment of death itself. But we don't want to remember that; therefore, we celebrate it as a day of birth. We arrange a big feast, invite friends and relatives to sing 'Happy birthday to you' or 'Long live so and so.'

"We think only of life. We never want to think of death because we feel that death is a complete annihilation, a complete destruction and dissolution of everything we think of as ourselves. We do not want to think about this dissolution. Yet the remembrance of death still keeps coming, and the more we try to forget about death, the more it comes. And the more frequently we think about death and the uncertainty of it, the more fearful we become. This fear robs us of our inner peace. Only when we realize the inevitability of our own death, will we feel an urgency to seek inner peace and true happiness. That is why in order to really live a life of happiness and contentment, one must learn to die. But, unfortunately, we do not know how to die in peace.

"People die all over the world in great pain, with great sorrow and suffering. Death is one of the most unbearable pains. Nobody wants to be in pain; thus, there is fear of death. Everybody wants to cling to this beautiful world, their body, their wealth, their friends and relatives, their home, and so forth. The thought that death will snatch away and annihilate all those things is extremely painful to them. So they die in pain and sorrow, because they do not want to leave these things. They want to cling to life and this creates a great struggle within. This struggle is the cause of severe pain while dying because they are not willing to let go. Many people are unconscious while dying, but within them there is struggle, conflict, and helpless fighting against death as it takes place.

"Children, do not die unconsciously. Learn to die consciously. If you learn to die consciously, you can decide what you should be, where you should be and how you should be in your next life. Or if you do not want to come at all to this world, that too is possible.

"Amma has heard of a Mahatma who was poisoned to death. He accepted the poison smilingly and keenly listened to the jail warden who instructed him on how to drink it. His hands did not tremble. He had no anxiety or fear of death. Coolly and calmly he sipped the poison with a prayer. As he was lying waiting for death, he even described how the poison was working in his body. He died consciously, not unconsciously. This is real dying, real death. Real death happens only when you witness the death of your body. For such a person death is a real experience. Man is consciousness, therefore he must learn to live and die in consciousness."

Mother's words on conscious death recall the time in Devi Bhava when Sugunanandan, Her father, demanded that Devi leave his daughter's body. In those early days he and many of the villagers were totally ignorant of Mother's oneness with the Supreme Absolute. They believed that She was possessed by Krishna and Devi three days a week during the Bhava Darshans and that the rest of the time She was crazy. "I want my daughter back!" he shouted at Mother during Devi Bhava. Mother replied, "If I give you back your daughter, She will be nothing but a corpse and will soon be decomposing and you will have to bury Her!" Sugunanandan continued to demand the return of his daughter, and the Mother said, "If that's the case, here is your daughter. Take her!" Instantly the Holy Mother fell down on the spot. Her body became stiff, her heart stopped beating and there was no breathing. She was dead from every appearance. Full of remorse, Sugunanandan implored the Divine Mother to bring his daughter back to life. The devotees who came for the Bhava Darshan were stricken with grief and prayed fervently. Eight hours passed before there was a slight movement in Her body, and She returned to life."

Here, then, is Mother's own example of dying consciously and re-entering the body consciously. Once you learn how to die you can choose your birth and death. It is perfectly under your control.

"Children, learn to die in bliss. Just as you celebrate your birthday, let death and dying become a moment of great celebration and bliss. Learning to die in bliss is meditation. This can happen only if you learn to cease to cling while living. Through meditation you can exercise ceasing to cling, ceasing to grasp. Your entire life should be a preparation to die happily, for only when you have learned to be willing to face death happily can you live life happily. Because then you will realize that death, like life, is also a truth. You will realize that death is not complete annihilation, but complete freedom from the grip of ego.

"Children, learn to accept death, welcome death, and say hello to death. Be friendly with death and death will become your friend. Once you learn to receive death, fears of all kinds disappear, and you will begin to live in real peace.

"The next moment is not ours. Only thepresent belongs to us. Living in the present, dropping the past, and forgetting the future is real life. We do not know whether we will be here in this body in the next moment. We do not know whether we will need the things and objects we use now in the next moment. We may breathe out and may never breathe in again. Who knows whether we will wake up tomorrow? The great saints and sages always lived moment-to-moment. They never planned for the future.

"Only a person who leads a moment-to-moment life can be completely free from fear. He alone can embrace death peacefully. This moment-to-moment living is possible only through meditation and doing spiritual practices. When there is ego, there is fear of death. Once the ego is transcended, one becomes egoless and the fear of death also disappears. In that state, death becomes a great moment of celebration. For those who live moment-to-moment, death is not a fearful experience; on the contrary, it becomes a peaceful and loving experience.

"When death comes, we are helpless. The constant remembrance of the possibility of death is the best way to learn humility. Humility is surrender; surrender is bowing low to all existence. Then there can be no ego. Once you become egoless, there is no more death. An egoless person cannot die, because he is not a body anymore. He is consciousness. Only people who are identified with the body will die."

Mother's profound satsang about moment-to-moment living, how to die and how the moment of death can become a great moment, a blissful experience, makes us recall the greatUpanishadic declaration, *'Eha atraiva'*, which means, Realization of the Self is here, right now, this very moment.'

A devotee asked another question, "Amma, what is the best way to drop the ego and embrace death lovingly?"

Mother said, "Trust. Simplytrust in the Guru's existence. Trust in aPerfect Master alone will help you drop the ego and all egocentric thoughts and thus enable you to embrace death lovingly. Live life beautifully. The beauty that permeates your life manifests in the beauty of your death. Yet, this beauty in life is possible only when you surrender to a real Master. Surrendering to a real Master is surrendering to the whole of existence.

"A real Master teaches you to accept everything that happens in life. He helps you to be thankful for both good and bad, right and wrong, enemy and friend, those who harm you and those who help you, those who cage you and those who release you from the cage. The Master helps you forget about the dark past and the bright future full of a thousand promises. He helps you live life in the present moment with all its fullness. He lets you know that the whole of Nature–everything, everybody, even your enemy–is helping you evolve and attain Perfection.

"When a person is thankful for everything, he will give up everything to lovingly embrace death with a beautiful smile on his face. For such a person, death is extraordinarily beautiful. For him, death is not an enemy to be afraid of. On the contrary, death becomes his greatest friend.

"Without knowing life, you cannot know death. For one who has not known life, who has not lived life in all its fullness, death is darkness; it is the end. But for one who has known life, death is the very heart of existence. Life flowers in death. That is why great masters, even though their bodies suffered, could die with big, blissful smiles on their faces. They embraced life with overflowing love. They embraced all of existence, all experiences both good and bad; therefore, they could embrace death also.

"This art of dying can be learned only by surrendering to a true Master. He helps you, your ego, to die in him, and he helps you to live.

"There is no guarantee for the future, for the next moment. Death alone is the guarantee of the future or the next moment. This moment is for you; the next moment may be death, who knows? Therefore, live this moment well. This moment alone is the guarantee. The next moment comes out of this moment."

It was ten forty-five in the evening. Mother asked everyone to meditate for a few minutes before they got up. Then Mother went to Her room, followed by Gayatri and Kunjumol. The brahmacharis, the householder residents, and the visitors all remained seated and meditated for about fifteen minutes as bliss permeated the air. Souls were stirred to great inward depths by the Mother's profound words. One by one all dispersed except for a few who remained meditating on the front verandah of the temple.

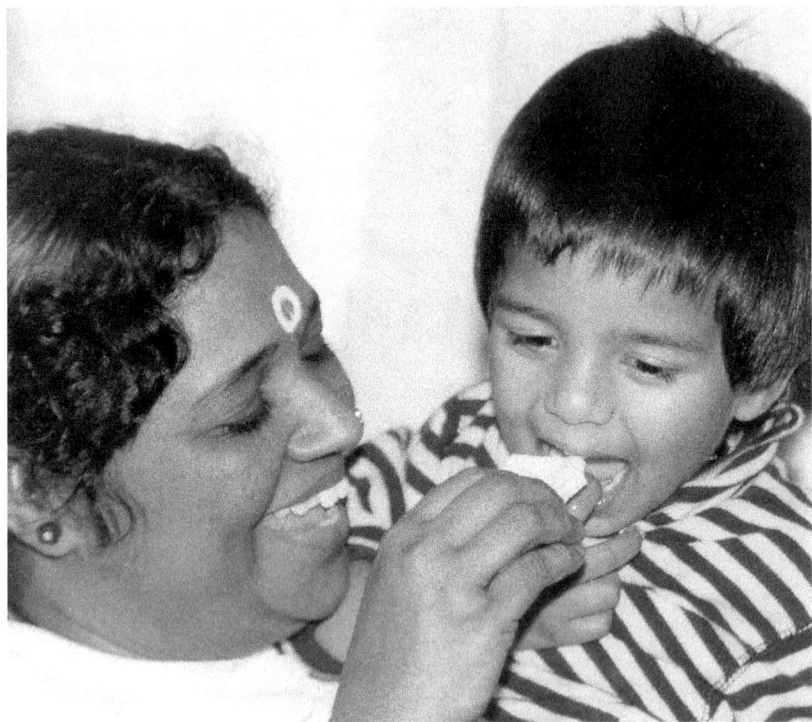

Chapter 2

Deluded by the ego

Thursday, 19 July, 1984

As the Holy Mother and Her Ashram became well-known, more and more seekers, including some belonging to well-established spiritual groups, came for Her darshan. Sometimes a lesson was provided by visitors passing through, as if Mother had brought them to the Ashram for that purpose alone. On this day a visitor arrived whose attitude and behavior were unusual for a spiritual seeker. He was a *sannyasin*[2] from another spiritual institution who had come to inform Mother about a fund-raising campaign the group had undertaken in order to raise money to build an educational complex. His band of spiritual seekers had started their march in Kanya Kumari, the southernmost tip of India, and they

---

[2] A brahmachari is one who has taken vows of celibacy and leads a life of spiritual study, austerity and practice coupled with service to the Guru. Through these means he builds the foundation for his spiritual life. He may remain as a lifelong brahmachari, get married, or become a total renunciate or sannyasi when he has attained the requisite detachment. The brahmachari wears yellow cloth to remind him of the perishable nature of the body which becomes yellow on the life force leaving it. A sannyasi takes lifelong vows of renunciation and celibacy and cultivates the attitude of oneness with Brahman, the Absolute Reality underlying the phenomenal existence of time and space. He wears ochre cloth signifying the burning away of all attachments which might bind him to identification with the body.

were heading north. On the way they wanted to have Mother's darshan and receive Her blessing for the successful completion of their fund-raising campaign. The swami who had come in advance of the group to arrange accommodation and food was not well mannered. There was an air of pride in his demeanor and in the way he spoke; he was neither humble nor polite.

At first the Ashram residents thought that his display of pride wasn't real, that he appeared proud because of a flaw in their own perception. But gradually the visitor's words and manner made it very clear that he was indeed full of self-importance. He made many demands of the Ashram residents and was condescending in his manner towards the brahmacharis who were trying to serve him. As he was planning to stay overnight, the swami asked for a room where he could be alone, but only a few simple huts with minimum facilities were available. Yet the residents made what arrangements they could and offered the best hut to the visitor.

Upon seeing the simple accommodations, he complained loudly, "What! Am I supposed to stay in this damp hut? I cannot stay here!" He stormed out. The residents were shocked. They wondered how a professed spiritual seeker could react in such a way, as they themselves were being taught not to place any importance on such trivial things as where they slept. The ashramites were in a great dilemma. Where were they to put the visitor? There were no 'comfortable rooms' in the Ashram; in fact there were no rooms at all, only huts. The residents and visiting devotees slept on simple straw mats on the ground, and there were many nights when the brahmacharis gave up their huts and even their straw mats to visitors and slept outside in the sand. It was therefore puzzling to them that a spiritual aspirant, especially a sannyasin, could be so demanding.

Finally, with the permission of Mother's father and mother, the residents arranged for a small room with a cot in their house.

But the swami was not satisfied with this room either. When he saw it, he made a long face; he left the room grumbling, and went straight to the hut where Mother was giving darshan.

Inside the hut, Mother was seated on a mat on the floor. Another mat was quickly spread out for the swami so that he might sit facing Her. The swami did not show any respect or reverence towards Mother; he did not prostrate, nor did he offer any salutation as a spiritual seeker normally would to a Master. As usual, Mother's face was lit up by a smile. The Ashram residents who had been trying to arrange a room for the swami were curious how this egotistical person was going to address Mother. They came to the hut and stood at the side and back doors to listen to the conversation.

Exhibiting an air of great self-importance, the swami said, "I represent a group of sannyasins who are on a fund-raising march. I have come ahead of the group in order to inform you that they will arrive here in a few days. The entire group wishes to camp here for a whole day. We will need good food and comfortable accommodations."

"Son," Mother said, "you have expressed the desire of the children in your group to stay and have food in the Ashram when they arrive. That is okay. Amma is only too happy to serve you. But it is not proper for you to demand comforts and good food. One who seeks the Truth should not demand anything. He should not ask for comforts and pleasures. A *sadhak* should feel content with whatever comes to him. A spiritual seeker is one who has surrendered everything to God. He should not expect any special privileges. You should be taking the journey you are on as an opportunity to learnrenunciation. Seeking comfort and pleasure should not be its aim."

"I don't agree with the idea that comforts and pleasures are prohibited to spiritual seekers," he answered back.

31

"An undisciplined way of living is most unsuitable if God-Realization is your goal," Mother responded. "Self-restraint is absolutely necessary for a seeker. It is important for you to study the rules and principles of spiritual life, but what good is study if you cannot practice what you learn? Those words become alive only when you constantly practice them in your life. If you are self-centered, giving importance to your own needs, how can you serve? An attitude of self-surrender and renunciation is necessary in order to serve others selflessly. Only then will everything you do become worship."

"Are you a person who has renounced everything?" he asked Mother.

This remark infuriated the brahmacharis and devotees who were already feeling annoyed. But because they were in Mother's presence, they managed to restrain themselves and did not move a muscle or voice any reaction.

Upon hearing the question, Mother laughed heartily and said, "Amma does not claim that she is a sannyasin, nor does She wear special clothes. Amma makes no claims. Whether you accept Her or reject Her, respect Her or show Her no respect, She doesn't care. But you want others to respect and recognize you. You wear ochre robes and say that you are a sannyasin. That is why Amma spoke to you in that manner. You should be setting an example for others. Asking whether or not Amma has renounced everything does not solve your own problem. What Amma has or has not renounced has nothing to do with you. You will benefit only if you change; and once you change, others will be benefited as well."

When the swami made no comment, Mother went on to tell a story: "There was once an old man who was looking back on his life. He sat in a tea shop with his friends, telling them his story. 'When I was a young man, I was arrogant and thought I knew it all. I felt I could do anything, and wanted to change everyone. I would pray to God to give me the strength to change the world. When I reached middle age, I awoke one morning and realized that my life was half over. I had done nothing, and I hadn't changed anyone. So I prayed to God to give me the strength to change those who were close to me since they needed it somuch. But now I am old and my prayer is very simple: God, please give me the strength to change at least myself.'"

Everyone laughed except the swami. He turned pale and was more agitated than ever. After a brief pause, Mother continued, "Don't try to change the world or other people before you are able to change yourself. If you try to change others without changing your own attitudes, it will not have any effect. Son, the purpose of this colored cloth is not to enhance your personality or make you look beautiful. It should be a constant reminder of the highest goal of human birth. It is not to boost your ego, but to help you become egoless. You feel proud to be a sannyasin. But the very word '*sannyasa*' means to give up, to give up your false sense of pride and self-importance. Try to respect the ochre cloth by humbling yourself. Try to have some more control over your own mind."

The swami was adamant, "I don't agree with any of these ideas. But I don't want to argue with you either. Now, are you going to provide a room for me or not?"

Mother smiled, "Okay, you did not understand the point. Amma does not blame you."

She then called Br. Sreekumar and instructed him to arrange Mother's own room for the swami. The residents disapproved of this and began to protest, not wanting Mother's room defiled by someone they felt to be the very embodiment of arrogance.

Consoling the brahmacharis, Mother said, "Children, what does it matter if he stays in Amma's room for one night? Or is it that your egos can't bear his? After all, he is a messenger. He was sent to inform us about a good cause. We must treat him well. Let him behave or speak arrogantly. It shouldn't matter to us. Whatever happens, we must abide by the rules of conduct that are appropriate for our own spiritual aspirations."[3]

Though everyone else was very disturbed by the swami's blatant display of egotism, Mother was not the least bit bothered. She remained completely unperturbed. Reluctantly some brahmacharis showed the swami to Mother's room. As soon as he was settled there, he requested that dinner be brought to him. According to Mother's instructions, the brahmacharis gave him everything he asked for. Having finished his dinner, he requested that his breakfast be ready at seven o'clock sharp. He even specified what he wanted.

Not being able to stand it any longer, one of the brahmacharis protested: "Swami, you should not forget that you represent the tradition of the great saints and sages of India. You should be setting an example for us through your humility and renunciation. But instead, you are making a big display of your ego and pride."

Momentarily taken aback, the visitor did not answer right away. But he soon gathered his forces and shot back, "Hey, don't you know who you are talking to? Don't you know how to behave in front of a sannyasin? You require a better understanding about *dharma*. Hasn't your Guru taught you anything? I presume that none of you have studied the scriptures. Tell your Guru that

---

[3] At this time, Mother's room was being constructed. Until then, She had been living out in the open under the trees or in a thatched hut. With increased crowds, the devotees felt that She needed some privacy and constructed a double-story brick house, the lower floor of which was used as a meditation hall by the brahmacharis, and the upper floor consisting of one room, a porch and a bathroom, was used by Mother. For a number of years it was the only living space made of brick, all the rest being thatched huts. Even after completion of the room, Mother did not move into it. She only occasionally used it until a year or so after completion when She moved in permanently.

She should make arrangements for you to study them. You need someone like me to instruct you in the scriptural texts."

The brahmacharis could not remain silent any longer. "Swami, if studying the scriptures is going to cause great harm to us as it has obviously done to you, we would rather stay away from such study."

The swami now raised his voice: "Are you mocking me?"

"No, swami, we are not mocking you," answered the same brahmachari. "It's only that we have a hard time understanding you. You say that we should learn the scriptures to have a better understanding about dharma. You say you have studied all the scriptures, and yet we do not see any right conduct in your actions. You are not practicing those *acharas*, and this confuses us."

"I am beyond the scriptures and acharas," answered the swami.

Shocked and appalled by such shamelessness, the brahmacharis didn't know how to respond. How could this swami claim that he was beyond the scriptures? After a long pause, one brahmachari spoke, "Swami, we know that you have a spiritual master. Do you consider him as a great soul and take his words as being as valid as the scriptural statements?"

"Yes, of course." the swami replied. "He is my Guru and a great soul. I must have faith in his words."

Without another word, the brahmachari who had been speaking with the swami rushed out and returned a few minutes later with a letter. Handing it to the swami, he said, "Be kind enough to go through this letter. It is from your Guru."

The ashramites expected the letter to bring about some change in the swami's attitude, for it had been written to one of the brahmacharis by the swami's Guru, and clearly expressed the Guru's great admiration and reverence for Mother. He had concluded the letter with this sentence: "Everything is Mother's *leela*; I humbly bow down at Her feet." Full of hope, the brahmacharis watched as the swami read the letter. He turned pale, but the next moment, to everyone's surprise, the swami raised his head and said, "I am beyond even the Guru."

What a shock! The brahmacharis were dumbfounded. Stunned by the swami's outrageous statement, they could find nothing to say, and silently left the room. As a group, they walked slowly to the temple where Mother was holding Devi Bhava darshan. The swami remained in his room for the entire evening, and did not come down for Mother's darshan.

Friday, 20 July, 1984

The following morning, when Mother came to the darshan hut, the swami pushed his way in and demanded to speak with Her. Mother smiled and lovingly spread a mat on the floor, inviting him to sit. With a stern expression on his face he took his seat. Mother sat on the other end of the mat facing him. All those present were captivated by Mother's humility and the serene divinity She radiated. But the swami was a hard nut to crack. As if to challenge Mother's immense presence, he once again revealed his arrogance.

The swami spoke, "As you know, I am from a highly reputed spiritual organization. I have been studying *Vedanta* at the Mission's Headquarters. After the completion of scriptural studies, I was initiated into sannyasa by my Guru. Since then I have been traveling around teaching Vedanta. Countless people have been inspired by my spiritual discourses. Many people tread the path of spirituality drawing inspiration from my teachings. Yet it seems that these boys have not understood me. They are unaware of my spiritually advanced state and have not honored me properly."

Hearing him boast, the ashramites were stunned and at the same time angered. Such a display of pride and arrogance was unheard of, especially in front of the Divine Mother. They all looked at Mother, but Her calm and unperturbed mood reminded them to keep their mouths shut.

As if listening to a misguided child's foolish prattle, Mother smiled at the swami. Very softly and gently She replied, "Son, calm down. Relax. You have studied the scriptures and you know what it means to be spiritual. But the saints and sages through whom the *Vedas* and *Upanishads* have come into being were totally free from ego. To be truly spiritual means to be egoless. These teachers never declared that they were beyond everything. They never said that they were great. They never demanded that others should worship, honor, or even respect them. It is because of their greathumility and renunciation that they are still remembered and adored. If you can stop insisting that others should respect and honor you, honor and respect will come to you unasked. Just try to be humble and patient and you will see how things around you change. Just try to be yourself. When you stop demanding, others will start honoring and worshipping you, even if you don't care, even if you don't want it.

"My son, you talk so childishly. People mock you. They consider you ignorant and immature. They don't pay any attention to you or give any importance to what you say. They think you are a fool. By feeling so proud of yourself and speaking so arrogantly, you bring disgrace and a bad reputation to your Guru and the organization you represent. You are the mirror in which the greatness of your Guru and the organization should be reflected. Let your words and deeds add splendor and glory to your Guru and to the work that he does.

"Try to be like a child. Only then will you be able to learn and grow. The feeling that you are grown-up or great will not help you to learn. Only humility will help you to grow. A child grows emotionally and intellectually because there is no ego to protest and create blocks. Knowledge flows into the child unimpeded.

But once your adult ego comes creeping in, the feeling of 'I and mine' appears and any possibility of inner growth is obstructed.

"Now, son, you say that you are from a big spiritual organization. But greatness doesn't lie in size or numbers. A spiritual organization may be large, but its real greatness lies in the humility, patience and renunciation of its representatives. No matter what institution one may belong to, spiritual or otherwise, one should be humble and willing to adapt. Only then can one really grow.

"Nothing is fully grown at birth. Whatever is born must go through a stage of infancy before it reaches maturity. This is healthy growth. Take any object, any plant or animal, institution or country, it has to go through different stages of growth. There is naturally a past, present and future to everything, because everything exists in time. Therefore, it makes no difference whether the spiritual institution you belong to is large in numbers or long-standing in years. What is important is that its representatives learn to abide by its teachings, especially if the representative is a spiritual seeker who has studied the scriptures. Son, didn't you mention that you have studied all the scriptures? So try to set an example for these boys here. Inspire them through your patience, humility and renunciation. Otherwise, they may develop an aversion towards scriptural studies. They are only beginners. If you are egoless they will accept and admire you; they will be inspired by you, and will try to follow your example."

The swami answered, "I am beyond all rules and regulations; I am even beyond the scriptures, and I have certainly not come here to set an example for these beginners." The stern look on his face remained unchanged.

Mother continued, "Son, those who have gone beyond have nothing to say. They know that this great experience is beyond words. Haven't you studied this great principle? Do you believe that the scriptures are mere words penned long ago by people who had nothing else to do? If you really believe in the Truth that the Great Ones experienced, if you really believe in their words, and wish to do a little bit of justice to this great spiritual tradition and to the ochre colored cloth that you wear, try to practice what they expounded.

"These children whom Amma is trying to bring up should be able to learn lessons of patience, humility and renunciation from people like you. But instead your words and actions have confused them; when you have gone, they will shower Amma with questions and doubts. Just last night they asked, 'How can a swami be so insistent about good food and comfortable accommodations? How could he sleep in Amma's room, knowing that it is Hers? We never thought that a spiritual seeker could be like this. We even feel reluctant to study the scriptures, if doing so will create as much ego in us as we have seen in that swami.'

"Somehow Amma managed to console them, saying that they should not find fault with others, for it will hinder their own spiritual progress. Amma also asked the brahmacharis, 'Why should you want to judge an entire spiritual lineage by looking at one person's faults? If he acts strangely, it is his own fault. How can you impose blame on the flawless saints and sages? How can you blame the entire medical profession for the wrong prescription administered by one doctor?'"

After a brief pause, the Mother continued speaking to the swami. "My son, you can act as you like, but do you know how much damage you are creating through your words and deeds? You have your own theories and concepts. That is all right. Keep them if you are so attached to them, but why confuse others by spreading such beliefs? That is a grave sin for which you will have to pay at some point. Amma teaches the children *tyaga* not *bhoga*, renunciation not indulgence."

A hushed silence fell over the entire hut. The swami showed no sign of emotion. Everyone watched and listened intently. When he finally spoke, the visitor's reply came as a thunderbolt: "You have repeatedly called me 'son'. Perhaps then I should call You 'daughter'!"

The swami's insolence was too much for the residents to take; one of them could not contain himself any longer, and he began to protest. But Mother stopped him with a gesture of Her hand. She turned quickly to the devotee and said, "What is the matter with you? Amma does not want anyone to interfere. Everyone, keep quiet until the conversation is over. Leave the hut if you can't do this."

If only the swami had been sensitive enough to see with his eyes and feel with his heart, he would have realized Mother's greatness by simply observing Her. Her unshakable patience and Her profound humility, devoid of any ego, undeniable signs of an elevated state, shone through all that Mother said and did. But the swami was too closed, too blind. This arrogant attitude of the swami is a demonstration of a famous verse from the *Bhagavad Gita*,

> *"Fools disregard Me as one clad in human form, not knowing My higher nature as the Great Lord of beings."*
>
> (IX-1)

Turning to him, Mother smilingly replied, "Amma has never asked anyone to call Her 'Mother (Amma).' She has never insisted on it. But everyone does call Her 'Mother,' and She, in turn, responds by calling everyone, 'children.' Amma has never cared what people call Her. Devotees and spiritual seekers call Her 'Mother.' Some people call Her by the name given to Her by Her parents. Some atheists and others who are against Her use unflattering or insolent names. This doesn't bother Amma at all. People see things according to their own *vasanas*. The same person who is sister to someone may be daughter to another person and cousin, aunt or friend to others. How many births, how many bodies, how many wombs, and how many names and forms have we passed through before arriving at this present life? How many times and to how many people have we been a father, mother, brother, sister, relative and friend? So, my son, don't worry. It's not important. The body is changing; it's unreal. Call this body by any name you like. *This* (pointing to Herself) does not care."

Mother's mood seemed to change, and She began to speak from a point of oneness with Infinity, "*This* came from the unconditional." She pointed to Herself again. "*This* was bodiless. *This* assumed a form and manifested in this body. Some call it Amma, some Sudhamani, yet there are people who call it Amritanandamayi and many other names. But *this* remains the same, unchanged, unaffected. No one can pierce the mystery of this Being."

Her penetrating words and exalted mood seemed to move the swami. He turned pale and could not speak. The power of Mother's words and Her profound statement coming from the unimaginable spiritual heights in which She dwells made him speechless.

The swami tried hard to hide his astonishment, but within a few moments he was back to his arrogant self, and was trying to cover up his foolish remark about calling Mother "daughter." As he spoke his voice was flat and feeble, "I don't care what you call me. Why should I? I am Brahman."

Upon hearing such a ridiculous statement, everyone laughed. It reminded them of Mother's words, "Egotistic people sometimes behave like fools."

In reply to his statement, Mother simply said, "A mad dog is also Brahman, but does it have any discrimination?" Then She closed Her eyes and sat deeply absorbed for some time. When She came back to normal consciousness, the swami, said once again, as if nothing had happened, "Well, can you provide food and accommodation for the sannyasins and brahmacharis who will be coming this way on their fund-raising march?"

Laughingly, Mother replied, "Son, that has already been agreed. But it is your duty to convey your message in an appropriate and polite manner. With Amma you can talk in any way you wish; She is willing to forgive and forget. But you cannot act this way towards everyone. People and organizations place a lot of importance on rules and regulations. In a police station you cannot talk and behave as you like. Laws exist and there is a certain way of doing things. You must behave in proper and appropriate ways in front of an officer or before a judge in a court of law. This is also true of how you are to behave in a temple or a church. You should adhere to the rules and policies that have been established in such places. You cannot act according to your own whims and fancies. The institution you come from also has certain rules and regulations, doesn't it? You observe them, don't you?

"Don't you know that each place has its own dharma? Everything has its own nature. How can you insist that a place or anything should change its nature, that it should stray from its own dharma? Is it right to demand that a place should change from its natural course just because you or someone else does not like the way it functions? You cannot say that a police station should be like a market place, or a temple like a liquor shop. You cannot expect an ashram to be a five-star hotel. Each place has its own way of functioning, that is its nature, its *samskara*. If it changes its nature, then it becomes something else.

"This is an ashram. It has a way of its own. Amma is very happy to welcome and feed all those who come here. Amma most lovingly invites all the participants in the fund-raising group to stay and eat at the Ashram when they arrive. You have conveyed the message that they are coming, and Amma is grateful to know this in advance. But son, this is an ashram, not a hotel or a palace where you can have the best food and the best accommodations. That is not possible. Simplicity and humility are the goals of an ashram and of a true spiritual seeker. You cannot expect a seven-course meal and a luxurious stay here. If you stay here, everything will be simple. To demand hotel facilities in an ashram is incorrect. That is against the dharma of an ashram. An ashram is a place where spiritual seekers live - people who are trying to lead a life of renunciation. Those who know this will not expect elaborate accommodations. They know that the primary purpose of visiting an Ashram is to feed the soul. To feed the hunger of the body is only a secondary concern at an ashram."

"I know all these things. Didn't I tell you that I have undergone Vedanta studies for three years?" remarked the swami.

Gently teasing, Mother repeated what he had said, "'I know... I have undergone Vedanta studies...I am great...'" Then She admonished him, "Son, you have such a big 'I.' That is your problem. It was 'I' who studied everything. You kept on feeding the ego. In this way, the 'I', the ego, got bigger and bigger, and the real 'you' starved. What a shame! You studied the scriptures and now, like a parrot, you just repeat them without understanding or searching for their real meaning. Son, have you heard this story?

"A rich man had a fine collection of birds and boasted about it to everyone who came to his house. Once when he was showing some friends around the aviary, one friend remarked, 'But you don't have a talking parrot.' Immediately when the guests left, the rich man went to a pet shop and asked, 'Do you have a talking parrot?' 'Yes, of course,' replied the shopkeeper and showed him a parrot in a cage. 'Does this parrot talk?' asked the rich man. The parrot itself made the reply, 'There is no doubt about it.' Ecstatic with happiness, the man purchased the parrot, unaware that the shopkeeper was trying to tell him something.

"Anxious to show his friend who had made the remark about no talking parrot in his collection, he invited the same friends to see the newly-purchased parrot. Seeing the parrot, one of the visitors asked, 'Does this parrot talk?' 'There is no doubt about it,' came the parrot's reply. Amazed by this reply, another friend asked, 'What is your name?' The parrot said, 'There is no doubt about it.' Again and again the parrot replied, 'There is no doubt about it,' to every question it was asked. Realizing that the parrot knew only this one sentence, the visitors began laughing and teasing the rich man. Annoyed and angry, the man opened the cage and let the parrot go, saying, 'What a fool am I!' And as the parrot flew away, it said, 'There is no doubt about it.'"

Everyone laughed and the swami looked around questioning, "Are you mocking me?" He paused and then looked at Mother and asked, "Are sannyasins prohibited from enjoying the comforts of life?"

Mother laughed aloud, "Son, it is because of the renunciation of sannyasins and their simple way of life that the rest of the world is allowed to enjoy. The very existence of the world depends on the spiritual energy generated by sincere sadhaks through their *tapas*.

"In any field in life, when things are being done the wrong way by some people, there are others who are doing things correctly. This keeps the ball rolling. This is how society functions without everything being completely destroyed. Bad is always balanced by good; evil is always balanced by virtue; insults are balanced by praise; destruction is balanced by creation; indulgence, enjoyment and attachment are balanced by renunciation, abstinence and detachment. While those who live in the world drain all their energies through over-indulgence and pleasure-seeking, spiritual seekers conserve energy by refraining from over-indulgence and inordinate attachment. On one side all the energies are dissipated, and on the other, they are conserved. Saving is a help to spending. Without saving, how can one spend? The tapasvi, the spiritual seeker, who practices austerities and conserves energy, is in due course, through rigorous spiritual practices, transformed into an inexhaustible power source. He becomes an inexhaustible source of energy. On the other hand, people who live in constant indulgence, with never-ending expectations, dreams and hopes, build castles in the air. They drain all their energies and finally break down. Then to whom can they turn? Who can help energize and revitalize them? Their only source of support is a spiritual person who has conserved a vast amount of energy, who can afford to spend lavishly from his limitless supply. He saves energy for the sake of others, for the sake of the world, and helps those who are in need."

After a short pause, Mother continued, "Asannyasin is one who, having renounced all attachments, is blissful in all circumstances. He is beyond everything. He has great patience, forbearance, perseverance and forgiveness. Dwelling in his own Self, he is not affected by time and place and finds happiness within. He can be in the lowest hell and still be happy. He can live in a dense forest full of ferocious wild animals and continue to feel blissful.

"Haven't you studied the *Ramayana*? Rama renounced his entire kingdom with a smile on His face, without feeling the least hatred or anger towards those who had conspired against him. The night they left Ayodhya, Rama, Sita and Lakshmana had to sleep out in the open without a shelter. Yet Rama found no difficulty in sleeping on the bare ground. In fact, he was the only one who slept soundly. Lakshmana and Sita were so agitated that they did not get one wink of sleep. Rama was a real sannyasin. Remember, He was a prince and had all the luxuries of life at His disposal until the day He left. But He had no difficulty in renouncing the royal pleasures and accepting a very unpleasant situation. Could youdo that? You ask, 'Can't a sannyasin enjoy life?' Of course, why not? But do you have the mental maturity and detachment to renounce anything at any time, and to accept andembrace something which happens to you quite unexpectedly? If so, you can really enjoy life.

"Son, this is not the first time a sannyasin has visited the Ashram. Many sannyasins and spiritual people have come here. The children here always serve them and do whatever is necessary for them. They are happy to serve the guests, and they have great reverence for sannyasins. They respect the ochre cloth. But your ways are strange and unheard of for a sannyasin. You have confused them. They are not perfect souls. They have the expectation that people like you should serve as an example; they need hints and experiences which will help them with their inner growth. But your strange ways and selfish words have shocked them. The ochre cloth that you wear should remind you to cultivate humility and patience in your every word and action. When people do not see such qualities in you, they will simply ignore you, considering you totally unfit for this path."

Obviously very agitated, the swami was completely silent. Mother closed Her eyes and remained indrawn for some time. The swami was sitting with his head bent in shame, staring at the ground. Yet every now and then he lifted his head slightly and glanced at Mother's blissful countenance, perhaps attracted by Her ecstatic mood. After a while Mother opened Her eyes. As if She understood what the swami was experiencing, as if witnessing his internal battle with the ego, She smiled benignly at him and continued to speak.

"Son, once a seed becomes a big tree with an abundance of fruit, it doesn't have to declare to the world, 'Look everyone, look at me. I am a beautiful tree, laden with fruit. Come, people, come!

Rest in the shade of my limbs! Enjoy the cool breeze that filters through my leaves! Enjoy my delicious fruit!' Even without any kind of announcement people will flock to the tree to enjoy its fruit, its shade, and the breeze. But first, like the seed coming out of its shell, you must come out of the hard shell of the ego. Just as the seed bows low beneath the soil in order to grow into a tree, so you, if you are to evolve into the Self, must bow low to all of existence in utterhumility.

"Take the example of a flower. In the bud stage the beautiful color of the petals and the sweet fragrance of the flower are invisible and unknown to us. But they are there inside the flower in their unmanifested form. They are dormant. When the flower blossoms, the beautiful color of the petals can be seen and the fragrance spreads all around. In the same way, divinity is in you. You are the Divine in unmanifested form. Eternal beauty and divine fragrance are potent within you. But just like an unopened flower, your heart is closed right now from your false sense of pride; because of this, you have not realized your true existence in Consciousness. Throughspiritual practice the flower bud of your heart will eventually open up its petals. Only then will you realize your identity with Supreme Consciousness.

"You cannot get milk from the picture of a cow, nor can you quench your thirst with the water in the drawing of a river. In a similar manner, you cannot experience the Atman from the words of the scriptures. Studying the scriptures is like using a map to find the directions to your destination. The question of whether you have understood the directions clearly enough still remains to be seen. The directions can be misunderstood and you may be misled. In fact, as far as Vedanta is concerned, there is a greater possibility of misunderstanding than of understanding the philosophy properly. More often than not, the study of Vedanta will only help to inflate the ego. Unless the ego is removed, no one can go beyond the *Srutis*, the *Vedas* and the *Upanishads*. Amma's only suggestion is that you should start doing spiritual practices and relinquish your pride about being a great scholar. Otherwise, you are wasting your life. As you progress in your spiritual practices, you will come to realize the truth of Amma's words.

"And one last thing, Amma knows that you have not been initiated into sannyasa. You took this ochre cloth on your own."

Mother's words struck the swami like lightning. He was clearly too shocked to speak, and sat for a long time without moving. Was he contemplating what Mother had said? Did he realize how foolish he had been in front of Mother and the others? Did he feel ashamed at all? Everyone sat in silent anticipation of what would happen next. Without another word the swami got up and left.

Though the Ashram residents did not see him again, they later heard confirmation that the swami had indeed only been initiated into *brahmacharya*, that he was not really a sannyasin. With this news, which did not come as a surprise to anyone, there was a report that he was no longer traveling around giving discourses, but that he had retired to a solitary place to do *sadhana*. So perhaps Mother had made a bigger impact on the swami than they had imagined. Although he had annoyed and even angered everyone with his relentless arrogance, their hearts went out to the swami upon hearing this news.

When the swami was gone, Mother addressed the brahmacharis, "Children, that son was indeed very arrogant. But there is a lot that you can learn from him. Remembering how you felt towards him, you should strive never to behave in a conceited way. Even when one day you have studied the scriptures and people begin to show you a lot of respect, you should not deviate from the path of renunciation and humility. You should never look upon others as inferior to you, and demand services and respect from them." After a brief pause Mother continued, "Your minds are agitated, aren't they? Let us calm down before discussing or doing anything else." She than asked Br. Pai to sing a bhajan. He sang

Verumoru pulkkodi

O Mother, I am just a blade of grass.
I am nothing without Your Grace.
Oh golden-hued One,
Shower Your Compassion on me.

I am a form made of ego
And powerful delusion.
O Mother, please remove my sins
And dwell in my heart.

The song had a deep effect on everyone. They all listened carefully to the words, contemplating their own insignificance and how it was due only to Mother's Grace that they had been able to accomplish anything in their lives. Mother did not sing. She sat motionless and Her eyes were closed. When the song was over, there was a long and deep silence which no one was inclined to break. A few minutes passed before Mother opened Her eyes and smiled, as She looked around at everyone. Her bewitching smile reflected Mother's unperturbed and unshakable nature. How can Mother, who is ever-established in Her own Self, be perturbed by anything?

Mother's Love

Saturday, 21 July, 1984

Although the swami had left the day before, his visit was still on everyone's mind. His behavior had been so unforgettable that he would be remembered by all the ashramites for months and even years to come. The day's darshan was finished, and Mother was sitting in the coconut grove, surrounded by the ashram residents and a few visiting devotees. One brahmachari took this opportunity to ask Mother about the swami. "Amma, how could you be so patient and calm before that swami's arrogance? The lack of respect he showed you made me so angry. I think everybody felt the same as I."

Thus came Her motherly reply, "How could Amma get angry with one of Her children simply because he was a little naughty and stubborn? Amma felt only compassion for him. He is also Amma's child, even though he is ignorant of it. A child sometimes kicks and hits his mother, and he sometimes utters a bad word about her, but the mother patiently endures it. She will not hit or kick him back. The mother knows that the child is ignorant and that he has no discrimination. Sometimes while feeding from the mother's breast, a baby may bite. What does the mother do? She doesn't stop feeding the baby. She doesn't get angry and hit the baby for doing that. The mother endures the pain and lovingly continues breast-feeding her child. Out of her love and compassion for her child, the mother shows patience and understanding.

"When you are a mother, you cannot help but love. You can only be compassionate; you can only forgive and forget. That is why whatever is loving and patient is known as 'Mother.'

"The earth isMother Earth for us. Why? Because of her patience. Human beings are cruel to the earth; they have no concern or love for it. They exploit the earth regardless of the wonderful boons and gifts it has bestowed upon us. Still, the earth patiently bears everything and blesses humankind with immense wealth and prosperity. Therefore, the earth is Mother Earth to us and Nature is Mother Nature. All the rivers on the face of the earth, especially the river Ganges, render great benefits for the entire human race. They, too, are our mothers. But we do great harm to the rivers; we misuse and pollute them. Still they are patient and loving to us. Similarly, the ocean with all its resources and immense wealth continues to bless us even though we do it much harm; thus the ocean is mother to us. In India, the cow, too, is considered a mother. Thousands of cows are slaughtered around the world by wicked and greedy humans, but cows still give us milk. And God is the greatest of all mothers because He, who is also She, is the Governor and Governess of the entire universe. Out of His/Her all-consuming love and compassion He/She instructs and inspires all these beings of the earth to be patient and compassionate to us humans, even though humans do not return their love.

"Therefore, children, Amma cannot be angry with anyone because all are Her children. Amma cannot see any differences. She beholds everything as Her own Self, an extension of Herself in different forms.

"Children, do not feel bad, angry or agitated about how egotistically that son behaved. Anger is very destructive. If you watch an angry man, you can see that he remains angry almost all the time. Sometimes the anger shows more and sometimes less, but it is constantly boiling within him. He cannot see or appreciate the good in others. Even if a person does a good job on something, he cannot congratulate him. Being tight and rigid, he cannot show or express love. He cannot even be friendly. With just the slightest excuse he can go into a rage. Such is the case of a jealous person as well, always ready to find a reason to be jealous, no matter how silly the reason. If nothing is happening to make him react withjealousy or anger, he will search for something to be jealous or angry about.

"An angry husband or a jealous wife can destroy an entire family and the children's lives too. Whoever comes in contact with them will be poisoned by their anger and jealousy. Fighting and suspicion are the trademarks of such people. Here is a story for you.

"There was a wife who was always so suspicious of her husband that they fought every day. Immediately when the husband came home from work, she would search his pants and shirt pockets, closely investigating and smelling his clothing. Each day she would look straight into his eyes to see if he had any fear or guilty conscience. She would look through each and every page of his diary. Sometimes she found a new phone number in his diary or a long hair on his shirt, and she would get suspicious and demand to know whose phone number it was or where the hair came from. Fighting would ensue with accusations, shouting and crying. This became a daily routine.

"One day the wife could not find anything, not even a hair. She kept on searching for a long time but still could not find anything. Finally she collapsed and started crying. The husband asked, 'Now, why are you crying today? There wasn't even a single hair on my coat.' Through tears the wife replied, 'I'll tell you why I am crying. Now you have started going out with bald women. I knew this would happen!'" Laughter filled the air, and Mother also laughed along with the devotees.

Study of scriptures

One householder resident asked, "Amma, if studying the scriptures can create so much ego and anger in a person, I don't want to study them. I do not want to harbor anger and cause harm to society."

Mother answered, "Study of the scriptures does not necessarily create more ego in you. It is wrong understanding of the scriptures that creates a big ego in a person. Scriptural study is not the mere gathering of information about the Atman, or the Self. You cannot collect information about something beyond words and beyond the mind, about something incomprehensible. You can gather information about people, objects, places in the world and how to do things like computer programming, which are products of human intellect. But you cannot gather information about Consciousness. You can understand Pure Consciousness only if you drop your intellect and reasoning. Study of the scriptures is to help you drop the ego and go beyond all explanations and interpretations. It is to prove the insufficiency of words, to explain that state fully. Study of the scriptures is to give you only an idea about spirituality. It explains the benefits of spiritual life. They are just explanations and conclusions. But remember, all scriptural statements and declarations have been made by those who have gone beyond the ego. To know the truth of the scriptural declarations one must drop one's ego.

"Information and knowledge block the mind from experiencing Truth. The mind and thought waves interfere with true experiencing. Suppose you want to experience the beauty of a flower. To truly experience you need to stop interfering with mental interpretations. Just look at the flower and you will experience its beauty. In the same way, the real meaning of the scriptures can only be known in silence of the mind, then you will really learn them and experience their fullness. To stop the mind from judging is real understanding. Study the scriptures but do not think they are all there is. Do not think that there is nothing beyond just studying the scriptures. Studying the scriptures must be accompanied by spiritual practices. Truth cannot be explained or interpreted. Truth can only be experienced. There is no harm in studying the scriptures with this attitude. Study the scriptures, yet remain as ignorant as a child. Then you will grow internally."

After a brief pause, Mother said: "Have you heard this story? There was once a Mahatma who, after accepting a young man as his disciple, told him to write down everything he knew about spiritual life. The Mahatma said, 'You must try to write down everything you know about religion and spirituality. This will be a very good thing for you to do.' The obedient disciple left and did as he was instructed. More than a year later, he finally completed the task and returned to the master with a very thick book under his arm. As he gave the book to the master, he said, 'I have worked very hard on this for a year, trying to put down everything I could think of regarding spirituality and religion. The task you gave me is far from complete, but I felt it would be best to show you what I have done.'

"The master looked through the thick sheaf of papers and said to the disciple, 'You have obviously put much time and effort into this. It is a very persuasive, clear and precise discourse, but it is much too long. See if you can shorten it a little.' The young man went away and worked on this task for five years. When he returned to the Guru this time, he presented a document half the size of the first one. The Guru read it and said encouragingly, 'Very good. You have included the essential ideas and truly approached the heart of the matter. And your manner of presentation has clarity and strength. But it is still too long. Try to condense it a little more in order to reach the real essence.'

"Although he was a bit sad hearing this, the disciple accepted what the Guru told him and continued to work hard and long to reach the essence. This time he labored for ten years and when he returned to the master, he bowed low before him and offered merely five pages with all humility, saying, 'This is the distillation of my spiritual knowledge, the very core of my life. This is what lies at the very center of my reason for existence, what religion is to me. I am most grateful to you for having given me this teaching.' This time the master read it carefully and thoroughly. 'Excellent!' he said. 'You have truly arrived at this through spiritual work, but it is not quite perfect yet. You still need to present a final clarification.'

"Years passed and one day, as the Guru was preparing to cast off his body, his pupil arrived. Prostrating before the master, the disciple handed him a single blank sheet of paper and then asked for his blessing. The master joyously placed his hands on the head of his faithful disciple and bestowed the greatest boon of Self-Realization, saying, 'Now you truly understand. Now you know.' The disciple silently sat at his Guru's feet while his master gave up his mortal frame to journey to the final abode."

Mother paused for a while, then said, "Children, only the attitude 'I am nothing, I know nothing' will help you reach the final state. That alone will help the Guru's Grace flow towards you. Approach the scriptures with that attitude, and you will really learn the scriptures. And even after studying the scriptures, try to maintain the attitude 'I have not studied anything; I know nothing.' This will take you to the goal. Try to remain like a child throughout your life and you will really learn. Study the scriptures with this attitude."

Chapter 3

The omniscient gem

Monday, 20 August, 1984

The early days of the Ashram were special for all who came to be with the Holy Mother. It was a time filled with precious and intimate experiences for the first group of brahmacharis who treasure many unforgettable memories deep in the caverns of their hearts. Mad with love for Mother, they poured their longing into the songs they composed and sang with fervent devotion. Yet at the same time, many obstacles prevented them from having as much contact with Mother as they wanted. The antagonism of Mother's parents towards the brahmacharis added to the intensity of their pining to be in Her presence. So all the songs were full of meaning, expressing the longings of their hearts.

In the beginning Mother's parents thought that their daughter, Sudhamani (Mother's given name), was temporarily mad. They were concerned about the family's reputation, about what people would think, for they expected that one day they would give Her in marriage. Thus they were very worried about the young men who always wanted to be around Mother. They felt that the devotees and the brahmacharis should come only during the Bhava Darshan days and insisted that they leave the premises immediately after the darshan was over. The moment

Mother's parents saw the brahmacharis around Mother they would get very worried and try their best to drive them away. On several occasions Mother's parents sent the brahmacharis home without even letting them see Her.

While Mother's parents did this out of their concern for the family reputation, some of the older devotees tried to keep them away out of jealousy. They thought that Mother's love for them would diminish if the brahmacharis were always around. Eventually it became so difficult for the brahmacharis to pour out their hearts to Mother in person that they began to compose songs expressing their agony. The following song gives an idea of how deeply they felt their sorrows

Karuna nir kadale.

O Mother,
You are the Ocean of Compassion;
If You are not compassionate towards me,
Who else will give me refuge?

O Mother,
My heart is always waiting for You;
Will this day be lost in vain?
Will this day be lost in vain?

Let this human birth be made complete;
Bathe me in the cool waters of Awakening,
Remove my body-consciousness,
And let me merge in the Light of Your soft smile.

O Compassionate Mother,
If I should eventually perish
Devoid of Your vision,

The coming generations will conclude
That Your compassion is of no avail.

In the course of time, as Mother's parents and the devotees began to have a better understanding of Mother's transcendent state, they became more accepting of the brahmacharis. But this did not at all diminish the brahmacharis' desire to express their deepest longing through song.

As more spiritual seekers came to be with Mother, Her parents saw that space was needed to accommodate the visitors, so more property was purchased. Mother's family moved to a house situated on the adjacent plot, and the original home consisting of two small bedrooms, a living room, a kitchen, and a storeroom was transferred to the Ashram's name. The room next to the living room was converted into a library. On this particular morning two brahmacharis, Balu and Sreekumar, were sitting in the library composing a new song. Singing new songs to Mother during Devi Bhava had become a regular event. There was a new song almost every Devi Bhava night.

Sreekumar was concentrating on playing the harmonium while Balu was trying to compose the tune. They had outlined the melody for the refrain and were trying to learn that much by heart when, quite unexpectedly, Mother walked in. She stood still for a while, then seeing what they were doing, She suddenly became like a little child. Full of excitement and innocence, She exclaimed, "Hey, are you composing a new song without calling me?" As She said this, Mother started stomping Her feet on the floor like a stubborn child. Enjoying Mother's *Bala Bhava* (mood of a child), the brahmacharis looked at each other and smiled. As if placating a little girl, they said, "But, Amma, we just started, we have only set music to the refrain!" Totally identified with the mood of a child, Mother kept repeating, "No, no... I don't believe you! You intentionally didn't call me! I'm not going to speak to you! I'm not going to speak to you!" While repeating this over and over again, She sat down on the floor. She then lay down and remained like that without saying a word.

Even though in their heart of hearts they knew that this was a Divine Play and that Mother was the very embodiment of detachment, the brahmacharis felt concerned and a bit sad. Together they called out, "Amma... Amma... Amma... ," but to no avail. They promised Her that they would not do such a thing again, but their pleadings and appeals had no effect, so they simply kept quiet. As soon as they stopped their pleading, Mother shot up from the floor and started pulling and pushing at the brahmacharis. She snatched the song sheet from Balu's hands, pushed him down, and started to sing the song. To their amazement, Mother sang the melody of the refrain exactly as they had composed it. Not only that, She went on to sing the next verse. Verse after verse, She went on to sing the entire song in a most beautiful melody perfectly in harmony with the refrain. What Balu and Sreekumar had been trying to do for such a long time was now being done perfectly by Mother within a few minutes. The song was

Idamilla tala yunna

I am a wanderer
I have no hearth or home.
O Mother, give me refuge
And lead me towards You.
Let me not get tossed about in deep waters.
Extend Your saving hand
And take me to the shore.

Like butter poured in fire,
My mind is being burnt in this world.
If a bird should fall,

The earth beneath is there to catch it.
But for me, there is no ground but You.
You are my only Support.

O Mother,
I long to reach Your Lotus Feet.
Haven't I called Your Name?
I never thought
You would forsake this simple child.
Was I wrong?
O Mother, I do not know.

O Mother,
Bless me with a vision of Your Feet.
I am constantly yearning to reach them.
O Mother of the Universe,
Don't I at least deserve this much?
Tell me, when will Your presence
Light up my mind!

This incident, like countless others around Mother, seemed a clear demonstration of the great Upanishadic declaration, 'That Knowledge by knowing which everything is known.' The Guru is infinite. His knowledge is also infinite. There is a famous verse in praise of the Guru which goes like this, 'One does not have to study every branch of knowledge, for all knowledge and its import will dawn within, of its own accord, if one has the Guru's Grace. To that Guru's Feet I humbly bow down.'

An experience Br. Balu had during this period serves as a good illustration. He had a strong desire to play the harmonium to accompany his own singing, for he felt that if he could play the harmonium while he sang, it would help him to merge more deeply into the mood of love and devotion. He tried again and again to play the instrument but was not able to play anything more than the ascending and descending notes. One morning while sitting inside the temple he was going over his usual scales. Shortly after he had begun, Mother walked over to him and said, "I will teach you." She sat down next to Balu, and just like a teacher helping a child write the alphabet, Mother most affectionately held Balu's fingers and pressed them down on the keys. Having done this only once, Mother got up and left, saying, "That is enough."

Balu thought this was just another one of Mother's plays, another fond moment with Mother; he never dreamt that this one harmonium 'lesson' which lasted only a few minutes was going to make a miracle happen. The following day, Balu was inspired to write a song. As he was writing down the lyrics, the melody came simultaneously to his mind. Shortly after the song was written and set to music, he had a strong urge to play it on the harmonium. It was as if someone had asked him to play it. He brought the harmonium to his room, sat down, and began to play. To his amazement, Balu found that he was spontaneously pressing the right keys. He couldn't believe that such skill could have developed in such a short time. But he knew that it was Mother's Grace which flowed through his fingers. It was Mother's divine touch which enabled him to play the instrument and thus fulfilled his intense desire. And from that day on he could play the harmonium while he sang.

This is the song, *Nilambuja Nayane,* that Balu wrote while learning to play the harmonium.

Nilambuja Nayane

O Mother with blue lotus eyes,
Won't You listen to the cries
Of this sorrowing heart?
Is it due to the deeds of some past life
That I am wandering alone?

I have passed through the ages
Before being born again in this life.

Please draw me close to You with a motherly hug.
Let me curl up in Your lap, like a child.
O Mother, I may not deserve You,
But will You forsake this child for that reason?
Come and hold me close to You;
Envelope me in Your merciful glance.

The theory of karma

Wednesday, 22 August, 1984

One afternoon a group of educated men and women who regularly met for spiritual satsang came to see Mother. They were all sitting with Her in a hut. One of them asked, "Amma, spiritual science is based on the theory of karma. We all believe that one is bound to reap the fruit of one's actions, yet the theory of karma is difficult to understand. Amma, can you say something about karma and how it works?"

"Son, first of all, you must keep in mind that the theory of karma is a mystery and not easy to understand. You can keep on explaining it, but it will remain a mystery. The theory of karma is not for intellectual analysis; you cannot prove it in the laboratory using scientific instruments.

"You can go on listening for days on end about the law of karma, and you will still remain ignorant about it. Speaking and listening to intellectually convincing talks is like taking a drug, You can become addicted; it can become a habit. So be careful.

"Children, analyzing the law of karma is not so important. The most important thing is to get out of it, to go beyond the cycle of karma, which is caused byignorance.

"There is another difficulty in trying to give a proper explanation of the law of karma. Negative actions committed in the past may not bear fruit in the immediate future, and the same is true with good actions. We may see a person lacking in virtue who lives a seemingly pleasant life, and we may see a good person suffering for no apparent reason. This may seem to contradict the law of karma; you may even decide that there is no such thing. To see its significance, the law of karma needs to be examined and evaluated from a higher point of consciousness. Otherwise, you may scoff and just ignore it saying, 'It's nonsense.' To rise up and see karma from a higher level of consciousness, one needs to do spiritual practices and to have faith. Here the measuring rod is not the intellect; it is the heart.

"You can raise a hundred objections to the theory of karma. You can keep on disputing it. You may even find ways to prove that the law of karma is a fallacy; still, the law of karma is operating in your life. You are in its grip. On the other hand, you may prove that the law of karma exists, quoting several incidents and experiences. But have you really understood it? No, you have not.

"A non-believer doesn't believe in the theory of karma. He may believe in cause and effect as a scientific theory, but not as religious faith. For example, his parents are the cause and he is the effect; the sun is the cause and light is the effect. His faith in the cause and effect theory is associated only with what he can perceive, only with facts. He believes only in what is manifest. He does not have faith in the Absolute, in the unseen. If you have faith in the theory of karma, you must believe in the invisible hands of God. You must believe that the hidden power of God is the cause of that which is manifest.

"It is like this: What caused this lifetime, this presently manifested state? You say, 'Vasanas from the previous birth caused this life.' Neither your previous life, nor the vasanas from that life are visible facts; they are just assumptions or suppositions based on faith. So you have to believe in a past lifetime and in the lifetime before that. Again, after this lifetime there will be another, and after that, yet another and another. Thus, the chain continues. Yet, we do not remember our previous lives, nor can we predict what our future lives will be. So, what is this? Pure faith, isn't it? Unless you can view it all from a higher point of consciousness, you cannot accept the theory of karma. That is why Amma said it is purely faith.

"All of life moves in cycles; the whole universe is cyclic. Just as the earth moves around the sun in a regular cycle, all of Nature moves in a cyclic pattern. The seasons move in a circle: spring, summer, autumn, winter, then spring again, and so forth. From the seed comes the tree, the tree again provides seeds, and the seeds grow into trees. It is a circle. Likewise, birth, childhood, youth, old age, death, and again, birth. It is a continuous circle. Time moves in a circle, not in a straight line. Karma and its results must inevitably be experienced by every living being until the mind is stilled and one is content in one's own Self.

"Cycles happen again and again as action and reaction. Time goes in cycles. It is not that the exact events happen over and over again. Rather, the *jivatman* (individual self) assumes different forms according to its vasanas. Reactions are the results of actions performed in the past. It goes on and on. Death is not the end; it is the beginning of another life. As the circle of life turns around, the actions of the past bear fruit. We cannot say when the fruit will come, what the fruit will be or how it will come. It is a mystery known only to the Creator. If you have faith, you believe; otherwise, you deny it. Whether you believe or not, the fruits come, the law of karma operates. But do not try to analyze how or why, because the cycle of karma is as mysterious as God.

Karma, too, is beginningless, but it ends when one drops the ego, when one attains the state of Realization.

"Man evolves into God. Every human being is essentially God. Evolution from man to God is a slow process. It requires a lot of cutting, polishing and remolding. It needs a lot of work and requires immense patience. It cannot be done in a hurry. Revolution is fast, but it kills and destroys. Man is revolutionary; God is evolutionary.

"The circle of life moves slowly because life is evolutionary. Summer comes. It takes its own time. It is never in a hurry. All the other seasons–winter, spring and autumn–they all take their own time. The cycle is slow and steady. But do not try to analyze the cycle of life. It cannot be done. The seasons come and go as a fact in the empirical world. But still they are a mystery, an experience. Behind the mystery lies the invisible power of God. That power cannot be analyzed. Have trust in that power.

"Try to forget about the cycle of karma. There is no meaning in thinking about the past. It is a closed chapter. Whatever is done is done. Prepare yourself to confront thepresent. Don't brood over the past or over past actions. What is important is the present, because your future depends on how you confront the present. Only when the constant presence of Divinity fills your entire life are you in the present. Until then you live either in the past or in the future.

"The power of karma veils our real nature, while at the same time it creates the urge to realize the Truth. It helps us to go back to our real existence. The circle of karma is a great transformer if you have the eyes to see it. It lets us know the great message: 'This life of yours is the effect of the past. Therefore beware, your actions in the present determine your future. If you do good you will be rewarded accordingly, but if you commit mistakes or perform evil actions, such actions will return to you with equal strength.' And to the true spiritual seeker, the great message says, 'It is better if you can stop the circle completely. Close the account and be free forever.' All these descriptions, explanations of karma serve to restrain humans from doing harm to themselves and others, and to stop them from moving away from their real nature or God."

At this point, Mother stopped talking. Closing Her eyes, She began to sing softly to Herself. She went on for a short while in this way, while everyone strained to hear Her sweet voice. But soon Mother opened Her eyes and asked the brahmacharis who were seated near Her to continue singing the same song

Oru Nimisham Engilum

O man,
As you run after the pleasures of the world,
Do you experience one moment of true peace?

Without understanding Reality
Or the essential principles of life,
Haunted and deluded by the shadows of maya,
You will surely perish in agony,
Like a moth in a flame.

Throughout the long process of evolution
You have passed through countless different bodies
Of innumerable insects, worms and reptiles,
Plants and animals,
Until at last you have emerged
As a human being.

O man,
Think clearly and use your discrimination!
What is the purpose of this human birth?
Surely it is not to be wasted

In the pursuit of trivial worldly pleasures.
Remember, a human birth is a precious opportunity
And a great responsibility.

O man,
Without giving up your false pride,
Your desire to acquire and possess,
Your desire to enjoy and indulge,
Without attaining the state of eternal union
With the Supreme Brahman
Peace and bliss can never be yours.

A few moments after the brahmacharis had finished singing, Mother opened Her eyes. One devotee was extremely eager for Mother to continue Her talk on karma. Breaking the silence, he said, "Amma, it seemed that you didn't finish talking about the law of karma. Please, won't you say some more."

"Children, Amma will tell you a story. Once there was an old man who had worked very hard his entire life to build a farm for his children and his grandchildren. He carved this farm out of the wilderness and managed to survive seasons of drought, storms and pestilence. After many years of toiling in the fields and tending the crops, he decided it was time for him to retire and spend his remaining years sitting on the front porch and contemplating the universe. His son had a family of his own and was eager to be master of the land. So the old man let him take over, happy to now relax in his favorite chair on the porch after all those years of back-breaking toil.

"At first when the son took over the farm, he was proud that finally he was the master. He too worked hard and spent long days and years fighting the elements and working in the fields. Little by little, he began to resent his father's laziness as the old man would spend all day looking up at the blue sky or bouncing the grandchildren on his knee. His resentment grew day by day. He looked upon his father as just another mouth to feed, and the more he thought about it, the more he was convinced that his father was a tremendous burden. 'What does it matter that he worked hard all those years?' the son thought to himself. 'Times have changed. I have my own family to feed and take care of now. Why should I take care of him?' Thus he grew angrier and angrier so that by harvest time he didn't want to share any food with 'that useless old fellow on the porch.' In fact, he decided it was time to get rid of the old man once and for all.

"So, he built a large wooden box out of teak, brought it in a wheelbarrow to his father and demanded that the old man climb in. Without a word, the father bowed his head and did as he was told. The son snapped the brass hinges shut, wheeled the box to a cliff, and just as he was about to dump it over the side, he heard a knocking from within the box.

"'What do you want?' the son shouted. His father's voice from within the box was soft and gentle, 'You know, I understand your feelings. If you want to get rid of me, I fully understand. You think I'm just a useless old man. But, before you throw me over the cliff, just let me out of the box and then you can shove my body over the side. I'd save the box if I were you; your children may have use for it someday.'"

Everyone laughed at Mother's story and She laughed along with Her children. As the laughter subsided, Mother now spoke in a serious tone, "Children, our actions will return to each one of us, whether one is a non-believer or a believer. Man is a victim of his karma or fate, whatever you want to call it. You may argue or raise objections. You may even convince others that the law of karma is a logical fallacy. But all this verbal jugglery and speculation cannot in any way stop the law of karma from continuing.

"Amma has heard of a weapon called a boomerang, which flies through the air and eventually returns to the person who threw it. Karma is like a boomerang which you fail to catch most of the time, so it hits you. The only difference is the karma boomerang may not return immediately. It may come back only after some time. That is what the old man reminded his son of when he said, 'I think your children may have use for the box someday.' He was telling his son, 'Remember, my son, that your son will settle the debt and close the account with you.' This settling of accounts may happen now, during this lifetime, or it may not happen until some future life. We cannot say. But no matter what your philosophy or beliefs, it is bound to happen. Keep in mind that this old man was himself reaping the fruits of his own actions. He probably did something similar to his father or to someone else.

"This circle will continue until you stop reacting to the present, which is the effect of the past. When you can accept present experiences as inevitable, as the consequences of your own actions, and face them without any thought of anger or revenge, then the circle of karma will stop moving.

"You have already created the necessary circumstances for whatever events are happening. And even now, through your actions, you are preparing the ground for your future. When the time is ripe, your actions will bear fruit; you will find yourself helpless in the grip of your own karma.

"Many undesirable events happen in your life. You suffer without knowing why. All your attempts to earn a living end up in vain. Unexpected accidents happen and untimely deaths occur in your family. A certain hereditary disease may afflict your family, newborn babies are physically deformed or mentally retarded. Are such events accidental? No. Each thing that happens in life has a cause. Sometimes the cause is visible, and at other times it is not. Sometimes the cause is to be found in the immediate past, but in some cases it stems from the remote past. For example, a great musician may be born into a family which, if you were to trace several generations back, had no musicians at all. How does this happen? What is the 'cause' for a great musician to be born into a non-musical family? If it is not heredity, what could it be?

"Suppose you get up one morning and as you are walking to the bathroom, you find that you are very tired and weak. After climbing just a few stairs, you gasp and struggle for breath. You feel dizzy and faint. Without much delay you are taken to the hospital and you are diagnosed as having a kidney problem. Now, did the kidney trouble begin just that morning? Did it appear without any particular cause? No, there is a cause. The disease was there, but in a dormant state. The disease manifested its symptoms only that morning. Would you say that this ailment is accidental? There has to be a cause for it, hasn't there?

"Nothing is accidental. Nature is not accidental. Creation is not an accident. The sun, moon, ocean, trees and flowers, mountains and valleys are not accidents. Planets move around the sun without straying even an inch from their predetermined orbits. The oceans cover vast areas of the globe, without swallowing up the entire earth. If this beautiful creation were simply accidental, it would not be so orderly and systematic. The universe would be a mess. But look at the beauty and charm of creation. Can you call this an accident? The vast pattern of beauty and order that pervades all of creation makes very clear that there is a big heart and a great intelligence behind everything.

"Children, our past is not just the past of this lifetime. It is not just a tracing back from now to the birth of this present body. The past is also all the previous lifetimes through which we have traveled in different names and forms. The future cannot be seen either; it is not under our control. We cannot predict what will happen tomorrow. The truth of karma is therefore more a matter of faith than anything else.

"We must be alert and careful about what we do today because we do not know what effect it will produce tomorrow. The present is this moment and we always miss this moment. Moment-to-moment living, in God, in Self alone, will stop the law of karma operating in us.

"Children, once you realize the Self, your true nature, you come to know all about karma. The mysteries of your previous births will also be revealed to you. You will realize the secret of the entire universe, the entire creation. Until then, you keep on asking questions about karma, trying to arrive at your own interpretations and explanations. Self-realization alone will clear the mystery. But once you attain Perfection, you will know that the real Self was and is ever-present. You will know that the true Self was never born nor will it die, and that it is never subject to the law of karma.

"Of course, the law of karma does exist, but it is more an experience of faith than fact. A fact can be proven, but faith is the strong feeling of the heart which cannot be logically proven."

After the last statement, Mother repeated, "Shiva... Shiva... Shiva... Shiva," circling Her right hand in the air. Then She sat in a totally absorbed mood as one of the scholars chanted a few verses from the

Soundarya Lahari

O Mother!
The crest of the Veda
Bears your Feet as its crown.
May You be merciful and place those Feet
On my head also.

The water offered to Your Feet
Forms the river Ganges
In the matted locks of Shiva.
And the lustrous red powder on Your Feet
Lends its glorious light
To the jewels in Vishnu's diadem.

By way of praise
We offer our prostrations at Your Feet
That are a delight to the eye
Because of their brilliance
Which arises from the lacquer-like dye
Applied to them.

Your Consort, Pasupati (Shiva)
Longs to be kicked by those Feet
And is jealous of the Asoka tree
In Your pleasure garden;
As even that tree
Is a rival aspirant for such kicks.

When the chanting was over, another devotee asked, "Amma, sometimes a true seeker undergoes a lot of hardship and difficulties. Why does that happen?"

"Children," said Mother, "you may see a person, who really wants to surrender and become a devotee or a real disciple, undergoing a lot of difficulties and problems. This is because such a person is going through a process of purification. All their darkness needs to be removed. It is not only this dirt that you see on the surface, the dirt you are aware of; it is also the dirt that you cannot see and are not aware of. So when you start the process of purification, approaching it with an attitude of self-surrender, naturally all this dirt, both seen and unseen, both the manifested and unmanifested, will come up.

"The other day one of the western children told Amma that in his country they can purify and convert even drainage water into good drinking water. How do they do that? By removing all the dirt. Drainage water will have all kinds of dirt and impurities in it. Without removing the dirt, how can it be converted into drinking water? Similarly, now we are like drainage water filled with all kinds of impurities and negativity. Just as this dirty water is cleansed through several processes, we too need intense cleansing. When a true seeker or a devotee passes through this sometimes painful process of purification, which is really the exhaustion of his vasanas, a non-believer or a skeptic may use this example as proof that God does not exist. 'If God exists, why does he have to suffer like this?' such a person will say.

"The suffering and problems that you may witness in the life of a person, who is trying to become a true disciple or devotee, is actually speeding up his or her process of purification. Through the exhaustion of both the seen and unseen vasanas, the karmic bondage is being dissolved. What he wants is freedom from all worldly ties and his attitude of self-surrender makes this happen. A real seeker is trying to dissolve his mind and go beyond the intellect and body. Only a person who has been in jail for a long time can enjoy the bliss of freedom. Similarly, only a seeker who has undergone a Guru's disciplining is able to experience the freedom of Realization.

"This quickening may not happen in the case of a devotee who wants to keep his attachments, possessions, name and fame. His evolution will be extremely slow. You will see him living in the lap of luxury, enjoying life. But in this way he is adding more to his existing vasanas, which in turn lengthens the chain of his karmic cycle. Through indulgence and enjoyment, the distance to travel back to the real source of existence also increases; whereas by burning upkarma, the true devotee or disciple is returning more quickly to his true nature, the Self."

In a somber tone, Mother added, "Man is bound to go through the cycle. The law of karma is his day-to-day experience, but still he does not believe in it, nor does he try to transcend it."

In great wonderment the devotees and the scholars sat listening to Mother's profound words. There was stillness for a few moments. Many times in the past Mother would not even open Her mouth if a question about karma or life after death were asked. She would just put a full stop to the entire topic saying, "It cannot be explained. It is pure experience. It is too controversial." Or She would say, "You don't need an explanation. Try to escape from the cycle of karma rather than speculate about it." But now Mother was speaking at great length on the subject. Her words, real knowledge from the heights, invisible streams of truth pouring down from the original source, flowed like the rolling waters of the Ganges to the ears of all those present. One could almost touch the teaching, feel it, imbibe it, and carry it in the heart as a precious and unforgettable gift from Mother, a gift to cherish and remember and contemplate during times of hardship.

No one spoke or moved for some time. It was as if everyone had entered into a trance through the power of Mother's sweet words.

"Amma, this is something remarkable," one of the visitors eventually remarked. "Your words have helped to clear many of our doubts. Every Sunday a few of us gather at the house of a devotee. We discuss different topics, read from the scriptures and share our experiences of you. We chant and meditate. The law of karma and its effects has been one of our main topics of discussion. Now, it has been made clear to us. But Amma, I still have a doubt. You mentioned that man falls victim to the hands of the karmic cycle. Does this mean there is no escape from this law of karma?"

"No, no," replied Mother, "that is not what it means. For one who does not have faith in a Supreme Power or ideal, there is no escape from the grip of karma. A believer, knowing that he has to reap the fruits of his actions, will perform spiritual practices like *japa*, meditation and prayer. These practices and the good actions which he performs serve as a neutralizer. The good actions in the present nullify the effects of past bad actions. Faith in God or the Guru gives a person immense strength to confront the inevitable karma. Faith in the Guru or God serves as an armor, a protective force. Even though the karmic cycle operates, its effects will be very much lessened due to his faith. Here we are talking about a person who believes in God but is leading an ordinary life in the world. He may not be so intent on stopping the cycle of karma. He may react, get angry and commit bad actions. He may have desires and want to accumulate wealth. But, because he believes in God, he will also perform spiritual practices such as meditation and prayer; and he will do good actions, giving food to the poor, etc. Thus his actions are balanced. This balance helps him to overcome the difficult situations which arise in his life.

"But the way in which a sadhak, a true seeker, faces karma is entirely different from the way of an ordinary believer. A sadhak is not worried about whether the results of his karma will bring good or bad experiences. He is not worried whether fortune or misfortune befalls him. A true seeker puts all his energy into going deeper and deeper into his own consciousness. He doesn't want to bother about the fruits of his actions. Surrendering himself completely to the Divine, he concentrates fully on doing spiritual practices. He simply allows everything to happen in its own natural way; he does not fight back. He knows that his karma is like an arrow which has already been released from the bow. The arrow must hit the target. The arrow might hurt, injure, or even kill him, but for him it doesn't matter if that should happen. It is like the phonograph needle running in the grooves of a record. The song has to play as long as the needle of life goes through the grooves. The song may be a terrible or a good one. Either way, he has produced it himself; it is his own voice. He knows that he alone has to confront whatever he must, even if it is painful. He will not want to run away from his karma, because he knows that it is a process of purification and that it is cleansing the stains created by him in the past, in some previous life. He wants to speed up the process. He knows fighting back or reacting will lengthen the chain of karma; therefore, he remains calm. Also, in the case of a sadhak, karma cannot operate with the same power or intensity that it would under other circumstances or with other people. The power of his spiritual practices will create a protective force around him. And above all, the true seeker will always have the protection and Grace of the Guru. Therefore, even in the most difficult times, he will receive solace and help.

"Children, a real seeker closes the flow of the mind to the past and the future. He tries to confront the present intelligently and with discrimination. He accepts the present circumstances without reacting to them. Any reaction will lengthen the chain of karma; for this reason, he tries not to react. His sole aim is to stop the chain of karma and its fruits.

"One can easily overcome one's karma through the Grace of a *Satguru*. Obey the instructions given by a Perfect Master and you will emerge victorious from all trials and tribulations. Every human being is destined to pass through certain experiences, some good, some bad. But if you follow the instructions of a Satguru, you will come out of all such ordeals unscathed. Your faith in the Guru will fill your heart and soul with immense strength and courage. Even death cannot touch you if you have the Satguru's guidance and Grace."

Faith

"But Amma, everything depends onfaith, doesn't it? What about a person who has no faith?"

"Yes, of course," Mother replied. "Love and faith are necessary in order to have strength and courage. Faith alone can cause theSatguru's constant flow ofGrace to reach us.

"Children, there are many people whose faith is foolish. They do not have real faith. The question of real faith makes them suspicious and skeptical, and will cause a hundred doubts to crop up in their minds. They are unable to have real faith because they are filled with more fear and doubt than with love and trust. Yet, they have no fear or doubt about their television set or other perishable things. Even supposedly intelligent people place all their trust in things like their cars, televisions and homes. These objects can break down at any moment, yet people have great faith in them. What a pity! They have no faith in the imperishable Atman, which is their own existence.

"Now, ask one of these people to have faith in a mantra, a prayer or a meditation technique. Or ask him to have faith in a Mahatma or God. He will ask you a hundred questions. He will express his doubts and fears. He cannot trust them. He might say, 'You know, I have very little time to do such things. Not only that, I consider my work as my sadhana. Also, I do not think that these things really work. Nowadays, spiritual people do more harm to society than anyone else.' His excuses will go on and on. The fact is, he does not want to believe. For him, his car, house and TV are enough. His faith in those objects makes him feel happy. Now, isn't this a foolish faith?

"Children, let me tell you a story. There was once a man who was very ill. One day he slipped into a coma and everyone thought he was dead. So the undertakers took his body, washed it and placed it in a coffin. Arrangements were made for the funeral, and a priest was invited to perform the last rites. As the coffin was being carried to the graveyard, the pall bearers heard a knock coming from inside the coffin. They set the coffin down and opened it. Everyone gathered around as the 'dead' man spoke, 'I'm not dead. I haven't died. Let me out of this box.' But they said, 'I am sorry, sir. You can't be alive. The doctor has certified your death and the priest has also confirmed it.' Whereupon, they closed the lid and the man was buried as planned." Laughter filled the air.

After a brief pause, Mother continued, "Our belief in our televisions and cars, even our faith in the body that we carry around, is foolish unless we understand their appropriate place and significance in our lives. If you look around and closely observe people's lives, you can see that lack of faith is the cause of all their troubles. Without faith you have no feelings, no heart, no love. This is a universal truth; it applies everywhere to everybody. Without faith you will be full of fear. Fear cripples you; it makes you paralyzed.

"Placing much trust in 'qualifications,' in certificates and degrees, people have faith in a doctor's or a scientist's words, though the doctor or the scientist is stuck in the intellect, and therefore limited. But, because he has no impressive qualifications, they will doubt the words and authenticity of a Mahatma, one who has delved deep into the deepest mysteries of the universe, and has unlimited wisdom and power.

"A person who has no faith will be unduly sensitive and fragile. Anyone or anything can hurt him—even a word or a look will make him feel dejected and sad. He will tremble in the face of difficulty. He cannot think or act with discrimination. In a moment of weakness, such people may even end their own lives; whereas a person with faith can keep in good spirits all the time. No matter what circumstances you find yourself in, your faith protects you. Amma is of course talking about unshakable faith in God or in a Perfect Master, aSatguru."

"But, Amma, people who have no faith in the existence of a Supreme Power also live normal lives, don't they?" one of the visitors asked.

Mother said, "You may find people without faith who lead normal lives without many problems or troubles, and you may wonder, 'This person has no faith in God or a Higher Principle, but still his life is all right. He looks happy and seems to be satisfied with everything that he has.' But your observation and judgment are based only on external appearances. He may seem okay from the outside, but you cannot know what is going on inside. It is quite likely there will be a dryness within him and that he will lack a zest for life. He will feel a constant anxiety about his life, and will rarely be relaxed. Unable to have faith in anything, such a person can be very narrow-minded and loveless. Unable to handle even his own problems, he won't pause to listen to those of his wife and children. Impatient with others, he can easily get angry and hurt people, and no one will want to be his friend.

"People like this continue their way of living for some time until they become aware of their dryness. This realization will help them to finally turn to something that can fill what is missing in their lives. That gap cannot be filled by anything but faith and love. Life becomes full and complete only when the heart is filled with faith in a Supreme Power. Until then, the search for filling the gap will continue. We all hope to fill it with different things. We try to fill it by working hard. We grab onto objects and try to derive enjoyment from them. But this gap remains. Not only that, the gulf may get even bigger.

"Each object we cling to and each petty desire we fulfill is like a shore where we think we can rest and be still. Remember, each leap to a shore, each attempt to find stability in the world outside, actually increases the gap of our dissatisfaction. The time to return to the shore of our real existence is getting longer. Soon we will find all the shores where we hoped to rest are crumbling and sinking. All things we place our faith and hope in will one day prove useless and meaningless. That day will come sooner or later. Yet until then, we remain unfulfilled because of our lack of faith. We remain skeptical and rigid. But one day we will surely call out, 'O God, I am helpless. Come and save me. Help me! Protect me!' We will call out when we realize that all hopes end in hopelessness.

"The so-called intellectuals or high thinkers who deny the existence of God, and rely on the power of theirintellect alone, often consider themselves superior to others, especially to those whose faith in God is strong. But actually, they are the losers; they are the unlucky ones. By not having faith they miss all life's beauty and charm; but they do not understand that. Suppose you see a precious stone lying by the side of the road. What if you simply walk by without picking it up? You lose the opportunity to own it, don't you? You are the one who has missed a great chance. The gem will of course remain precious and priceless, and another person who recognizes its value will be made rich just by picking it up. Instead of admitting your mistake, instead of confessing your blindness, you will defend yourself, saying that the precious stone was a fake, or that you don't care about it at all. Skeptics defend their beliefs in a similar way. But God is not worried if human beings don't believe in Him. Those who are without faith in the Divine are the losers. Without love, such people lack vitality; they are like living corpses. The beauty and charm of life will not shine through people like this. Nobody will be attracted to them; nobody will feel inspired by their actions or words. People will not care about them. Even their own wife and children will find it difficult to put up with them. But the day will come when they will also call out, 'Help! God!'"

Surrender to face karma

The visitor asked, "Amma, is there a particular period of time in one's life when this law of karma starts operating? Is it possible to get a hint or sign before it happens?"

With a mischievous smile on Her face, Mother replied, "When the egoistic feelings of 'I' and 'mine' come up, that is when the law of karma begins to operate on you. When the ego arises, you forget God. You act and talk against the laws of nature. You degenerate in every way. All your virtues and good qualities, like concern for others, love and forgiveness disappear. That is when the law of karma takes effect. When you start brooding about the past, when you start criticizing and insulting others and blame them for the mishaps that happen in your own life, when you plan and dream about a future of promises and forget to live in the present, that is when the law of karma starts operating in you. Both in the case of an individual and in the case of society as a whole, this happens when God is forgotten. When God is forgotten, people enter into the cycle of karma. Certainly this life and the body itself are the results of karma. But there is an intelligent and healthy way to let karma operate in our lives, a way that can allow us to lead a happy and joyful life while confronting each karmic or predestined experience."

Another visitor asked, "What is this intelligent and healthy way of exhausting the karmic experiences?

"Never forget your true Self," answered Mother. "Never forget that your real existence is in God and all that you claim as your own is just passing. If this can become our slogan and if we can practice it in our everyday life, that is the most intelligent way to exhaust our karmic experiences.

"Never forget God. Never forget your real Source. Never move away from the real center within you. Can you do this? If so, you can overcome the law of karma. If this is practiced, karma and its effects cannot harm you. Karma becomes impotent through God's or theGuru's Grace.

"Without Grace one cannot confront destiny. Human effort is, of course, powerful. But human beings lack discrimination. They act out of egotism, and because of this, their actions are ultimately ineffectual in the face of destiny.Surrender to the *Paramatman*. Perform your actions in the world without feeling proud of your power; pray for, and try to feel, God's presence in all that you do, and be thankful for His Grace. This is what is most important. Human beings think that it is possible to oppose destiny. But they cannot. Try to fight with any amount of power and force, and you will be defeated. You will be completely disarmed. You will be crushed under destiny's weight."

A question followed, "Amma, are you saying that man is completely helpless in the face of karma or destiny?"

Mother answered, "No, that is not the point. The point is to face karma, confront it without feeling egoistic about your own power, but by invoking and relying on God. God's power can be invoked only when you surrender to Him.Surrender is becoming humble, being able to bow down low. Children,humility is the way. Bow low and karma will miss you; it will go over your head because you are the servant of God and thus protected by Him.

"Amma wouldlike to relate to you two incidents which happened during LordKrishna's life. Both happened during the great battle of Kurukshethra. Here is the first example. When Drona, the great teacher of weaponry for both the Pandavas and Kauravas, was killed by the Pandavas,Aswathama, his son, flew into a rage.

83

He was so upset by the treacherous killing of his father, that he shot theNarayanastra, the most destructive missile of all. Spitting fire and producing thousands of other destructive weapons from within, the powerful missile created havoc in the Pandava forces. Within seconds, thousands of soldiers were killed. Lord Krishna was the only one who knew how to avoid this great missile. He ran through the battalions of soldiers, instructing everybody to relinquish all their weapons and lie down on the ground. Krishna's command was immediately obeyed, and the entire Pandava force lay down, except for Bhima, the second Pandava brother. He remained on the battle field, shouting and challenging the deadly weapon. He did not want to surrender. He absolutely refused to give up his own weapons and lie down. Wanting to have a face-to-face encounter with the great Narayanastra missile, he boldly kept on challenging the missile and taunting Aswathama. Thus Bhima, one of the strongest men in the world, stood fearlessly in front of the arrow.

"Unfortunately the arrow was extremely powerful and proved too colossal even for him. The fire it emitted slowly began enveloping Bhima. Still, he danced around, shouting and jumping like an enraged fireball. Seeing the inevitable danger that threatened Bhima, the Lord andArjuna came rushing over, calling out loudly, begging him, 'Bhima, throw your weapons away and lie down!' But all their pleading was in vain. Finally, both Krishna and Arjuna seized all of Bhima's weapons and threw them away. Together they grabbed him and forced him down. The effect was immediate; the powerful missile withdrew and moved away from Bhima.

"Now, children, the powerful Narayanastra represents karma. Nothing could prevent it from attacking the soldiers; even the strongest and most powerful warriors like Bhima were helpless against its might. Only the Lord's command, 'Lie low, be humble,' could save them. Bhima was egotistic. He thought that through his strength, he could win. But he was attacked and almost defeated. He would have become a handful of ashes in a few moments, had it not been for the intervention of the Lord. Bhima had acted out of his own volition. He had put forth his own effort. He had tried to fight back. That was action, but wrong action in the wrong place and at the wrong time.

"The Lord Himself instructed, 'Lie low, abandoning all your weapons.' But Bhima was too egotistic to do that. He thought, 'I am great. I am powerful. Nothing can defeat me.' Most people are egotistic and think that they can do many things. But destiny is much more potent and will destroy you unless you are adhering to the words of a Perfect Master or God. Even then, the Lord saved him because Bhima was willing to surrender. He had always obeyed Krishna's word. So the Lord was compassionate towards him and saved him.

"Children, in the face of karmic experiences all your weapons of ego and strength are powerless unless you abandon them, following the Guru's instructions and throw yourself down in humblesurrender. You cannot escape karma. If God's or the Guru's Grace is with you, the arrow of karma, which has already left the bow of your past life, cannot hurt you."

After a short pause, Mother continued, "Now, listen to this secondincident from the same battlefield of the *Mahabharata*. In the fight betweenArjuna andKarna, Karna was far superior in wielding the bow and arrow. Intending to sever Arjuna's head, he shot a divine missile. LordKrishna, Arjuna's charioteer, foresaw this great karmic danger coming towards Arjuna. Immediately the compassionate Lord, pressing hard with his big toe, made all four horses kneel down. Also, the powerful pressure of the Lord's big toe pushed the chariot wheels a few inches down into the earth. This made the arrow take away Arjuna's crown without injuring any part of his body.

"Here also there are a few points to remember. First of all, the Lord himself was Arjuna's charioteer. This means that Arjuna chose the Lord as the person to hold the reigns of his life's chariot. Before the whole battle had begun, Arjuna andDuryodhana were given two choices. Krishna told them, 'I can give My entire army to one of you, but I won't come. Or I can come without any weapons as your charioteer, and the army will help your foe. Which do you choose, Me or My army?' Without any hesitation whatsoever, Arjuna said, 'I want you, Lord. You alone are enough. I don't need the army.' So Arjuna chose the Lord as his Master. Through his self-surrender, Arjuna could obtain the Lord's Grace. Arjuna knew how to discriminate. He did not choose human soldiers as his friends and helpers. He chose the Divine Lord alone to help him. That makes a big difference. The Grace of the Lord lets the karmic arrow pass over your head, maybe destroying an insignificant crown or something similar, but saving you from a fatal mishap.

"Arjuna was powerful, but not as powerful as Karna. Arjuna is action, human effort; Karna is the destiny in store for you. Karna was more powerful than Arjuna. But all of Arjuna's efforts would have failed to save his life from Karna's fatal arrow had the Almighty Lord's Grace not been there. You see, Duryodhana had a bigger and better army than the Pandavas. He had many great warriors on his side. His army was stronger in every way. Duryodhana and his army represent human power and strength without the aspect of Grace. The Pandavas had Krishna, the Lord, the very source of Grace and power, on their side. The battle was destined to happen. Nobody could avert it. It was the culmination of all the past actions performed by both the Kauravas and the Pandavas. It was the fruit of their actions. But self-surrender, faith, and devotion helped the Pandavas overcome the situation, whereas arrogance, wickedness, and egotism ruined the Kauravas. They easily fell victim to the powerful force of karma."

Mother stopped and then said, "Children, enough talking for now."

One of the visitors in the group was trained in classical Indian music and had composed several songs. He expressed a wish to sing for Mother. Sitting down at the harmonium, he sang

Paravasamannen Hridayam

O Mother,
My mind is deeply distressed
By many distracting thoughts.
Don't wait any longer;
Pay attention to this destitute!

Please know that I am helplessly falling
Into the depths of the sea.
O Mother, whose glorious past is known to all,
Won't You come and soothe my weeping eyes?

My mind is confused with countless waves of despair
I am floundering in a sea of fire,
Without ever reaching the shore,
Without having caught a glimpse Your Lotus Feet.

When the devotee began to sing, Mother closed Her eyes and sat in perfect meditative posture. The man sang with much feeling, and all who were present were obviously moved. As the song ascended to its peaks, the scholar singing through tears, Mother raised Her right hand. The ring finger and the middle finger were folded down and the rest of the fingers were held up straight in the gesture of a divine *mudra*. Her left hand rested on Her thigh and a beaming smile lit Her face. Even after the song was over, Mother remained in this state. Her divine mood inspired the scholar to sing another song

Ehi Murare

O Destroyer of the demons Mura and Madhu,
O Kesava, Ocean of Compassion,
The Friend of those who approach You with humility,
Frequenter of the forest groves,
O Blessed One, with a beautiful face,
Come to me!

O Krishna,
Serene Madhusudana,
There are hundreds of honey bees within the forest groves.
Krishna, my playful Beloved,
O serene Madhusudana,
I beg You for the gift of Your Darshan!

O Radha's enchanter,
Slayer of Kamsa,
O Krishna, I prostrate at Your Feet
That remove all sorrow.
O Janardana, clad in a yellow garment,
Come to me in the Mandhara grove!

Everyone responded to this second song with great love and devotion, some clapping the rhythm as they sang. A few minutes after the song was over, everyone left the hut as instructed by one of the senior brahmacharis. Having been transported to some other realm by the devotee's songs, Mother remained in Her sublime state for some time.

Chapter 4

Early in the morning near the temple verandah, Mother was consoling a woman from the neighborhood who was weeping and complaining about her husband. "Ammachi," she said. "Am I destined to suffer like this for the rest of my life? I have seven children. The eldest girl is still not married and she is already twenty-eight years old. My son, the fifth child, is very brilliant in his studies, and I am trying to send him to school. We need to create a better situation at home so he can concentrate on his studies, but my husband spoils everything. He doesn't work to support us financially, and he offers no emotional support either."

Unable to control herself any longer, the woman sat down on the temple verandah and burst into tears. Mother sat next to her and gently lifted the woman's head. She said, "Daughter, don't worry," as She wiped away the woman's tears. "Amma will try to talk to your husband. Let's hope that he will listen to Amma. If he continues to be disruptive and does not mend his ways, Amma will think of a way to help you. Don't cry. Be calm."

Putting the woman's head on Her shoulder, Mother kissed her cheeks and continued to express her affection and concern. The woman began to relax. "Ammachi," she said, obviously somewhat consoled, "he has a lot of respect for you, and has only good things to say. But he is not very reliable."

Mother replied, "Just let Amma try." She stood up and was about to walk away when the woman called out, "Ammachi!" Mother turned around, "What is it, daughter? Do you need something?" With a bit of hesitation she said, "Ammachi, there is no food in the house. There has been no work for me for the last two days. Until yesterday I could somehow manage with the little savings I had, but today there is not even a single penny in the house. Besides, my son who is good in his studies has a very high fever. I have no means to take him to the hospital or purchase any medicine the doctor might prescribe."

Mother smilingly said, "Why do you hesitate to tell Amma this?" After saying this She asked Kunjumol standing nearby to call Gayatri. Gayatri arrived in a few minutes and Mother whispered something in her ear. Gayatri left and while waiting for her to return, Mother began some light talk with the village woman.

Whenever Mother talks with the village neighbors, She becomes one of them and one with them. They feel so at home with Her that they pour out their hearts fully. They tell Her everything, from the most personal to the most mundane. Mother does not show any impatience. She listens attentively to all that they have to say and makes them feel comfortable and relaxed. Many of them are not devotees, and some don't even believe in God. Yet they are all somehow touched by Mother. After talking to Mother about their problems, one can be hear them say, "Whatever it may be, She gives great relief and confidence."

Gayatri soon returned with a cloth bag filled with rice, fruits, and vegetables. Mother took the bag from her and handed it to the woman. Turning to Gayatri, Mother said, "You give the money." Gayatri handed some money to the woman while Mother explained to her that it was to be used for taking her son to the hospital and for the purchase of any required medication. The village woman left the Ashram with a heart full of gratitude and love.

Live in anticipation of the Lord

Afterwards Mother went to the brahmacharis' huts, where She spent a few minutes in each hut, giving instructions to the brahmacharis about how to hang their clothes, how to keep their altar properly, how to keep their books and personal things in an orderly way, and other such advice. In one hut there was a brahmachari who was not very neat and did not keep the hut clean. Many of his things were lying around the room and the picture on the altar was full of dust. With a serious look on Her face, Mother turned to the brahmachari and said, "Son, is this the way to keep your room? Only a person who has no *sraddha* or *bhakti* will do this. Look at your clothes. See how the books are scattered all over the floor. Look how dusty this picture is, your *dhyana rupam* (form of meditation)."

Mother picked up the picture and showing it to everyone, said, "Look at this picture. This is the form he meditates on. Look how careless he is about the dhyana rupam. Can a person who has love for his Beloved Deity or his Guru do something like this? It is said that one should love one's Beloved Deity as much as one loves oneself." Turning to the careless brahmachari, She continued, "It is quite obvious that you have not cleaned this picture for a long time. This shows that you have no love for your Beloved Deity.

"Children, a sadhak is supposed to see divinity or the presence of his Guru or God everywhere. When a person tries to see and feel the Divine Presence everywhere, he will value external cleanliness. He thinks that his God, or his *Ishta Devata,* dwells everywhere, walks everywhere, and sits everywhere. With intense love and devotion, the sadhak waits with great expectation for His arrival. The seeker has unquenchable thirst to drink in His beauty, to fill his heart with the Lord's presence, so he anxiously waits. In each footstep he hears, in each movement he feels, in each and everything he looks at, he hopes to behold his Lord, his Beloved God or Goddess. He cannot offer a dirty and dingy place to his Lord. He cannot welcome Him to a place that is messy and not clean. The Lord is his Beloved. But he also knows that the Lord is omnipotent, omnipresent and omniscient, and that He is purer than the purest. This awareness fills him with awe and reverence.

"What do you offer to the person you love most, to the person who is dearest to you? What would you want to give him or her? Only good things. You would never think of offering anything bad to such a person, would you? No. So, the love and affection to the Lord, your Beloved Deity or your Guru, is reflected in your actions, in the beauty of your actions. This does not mean that God will accept only what is good. It is true that He will accept anything that is offered with love and devotion. But we have not reached that state of supreme love where everything, even your own individuality, is forgotten. In that state of supreme love both purity and impurity are transcended.

"Constant waiting, waiting with intense longing for the Lord's or the Guru's arrival is the sign of a true devotee. Such a seeker is always ready to receive Him; therefore, he is always prepared both internally and externally to welcome his Guru or the Lord."

One brahmachari asked, "Amma, could you elaborate on what you mean by waiting?"

"Son, waiting eagerly for the Lord should be a sadhak's constant mental attitude. Each moment you wait you should be prepared to receive and welcome Him. Your altar is not just a place to keep pictures; it is a special place for your Lord to dwell. When you have this feeling, you can never be messy or unclean. Even if your house or your dwelling place is small, even if it is tiny, you should keep it clean. Try to make it serene like a temple. The surroundings should also be kept in the same way. Your room should be rearranged, reorganized, and kept clean in such a way that it should look like you are constantly waiting to welcome your Lord. The remembrance that 'my Lord' or 'my Mother' can step in at any moment will certainly help you keep the room clean and tidy, for you will want to make it suitable for Him or Her to come in and be seated. Your mental attitude, your purity andcleanliness will be reflected in your actions as well.

"You have heard ofSabari, the great devotee of LordRama. That was her attitude. Every moment of her life she was waiting for her Lord. She thought, 'He might walk in at any time. So I should be well-prepared to welcome Him.' And she was. Sabari always kept her house and its surroundings beautifully clean. Every day she cleaned the room and kept the bed prepared for the Lord to rest. Each day she decorated the house, and not one day passed when she forgot to pave the pathway to her simple home with fresh and fragrant flowers. She plucked the freshest and choicest fruits for the Lord to eat. All the puja articles for the ceremonial washing of the Lord's feet were always kept shining and ready to be used. The seat for her Lord to sit on was beautifully decorated every single day. Sweet fragrance filled the atmosphere. Every morning Sabari made a garland with freshly plucked flowers. The Lord's name was constantly on her lips. With eyes fixed on the pathway, Sabari, the great devotee, waited and waited and waited, for long, long years.

"TheGopis also waited in the same manner afterKrishna's departure from Vrindavan. They went mad as Krishna was leaving for Mathura and wanted to stop Him. When king Kamsa's messengers, Akrura and Uddhava, came to take Krishna back to Mathura, the Gopis scolded them severely. So great was their distress that they held these two innocent messengers responsible for Krishna's departure and they cursed them for it. 'Don't worry. I have a mission to fulfill in Mathura,' Krishna said. 'Once that is done, I won't stay there a second longer. I will come rushing back to you, my beloved ones. How can I be away from you who are the very embodiments of love?' But Krishna never returned to Vrindavan.

"For the Gopis, Krishna's departure was the beginning of a long and endless wait full of expectation and hope. Each day the Gopis kept butter and *ghee* ready in their homes, hoping that Krishna would come. They decorated their houses and drew different auspicious diagrams and symbols in the front yards to welcome their beloved Krishna. Fixing their gaze on the entrance gate, the Gopis waited every day. After Krishna's departure their eyes were always filled with tears. For them, all the aspects of nature–the animals, birds, trees, bushes, plants, creepers, flowers, rivers, mountains and valleys–were all waiting for Krishna. Finally, their longing transformed them into *Krishnamayis*; they were totally permeated with Krishna.

"Children, this is why Amma said you have no love orfaith. If you had, you would have been ready and waiting to welcome your Beloved Deity, or Amma, at any time. If that were the case, this room would not have been such a mess. It would have had the serenity and purity of a temple. This shows your lack ofsraddha andbhakti which are the most basic qualities that asadhak should have."

Mother took the photograph, and using the end of Her sari, wiped off the dust. After placing it back on the altar, She then began to pick up the clothes and books lying on the floor. As She put the books on a small corner shelf, She said, "Look here, he took the books from this shelf but never bothered to put them back." Next She asked one of the brahmacharis for some rope. While waiting for the rope to be brought, Mother all of a sudden turned around and spoke to the brahmachari who had stayed in the room, "Perhaps you're thinking, 'Why is Amma creating such of an uproar over such a silly matter?' You are thinking that it is the heart that needs to be purified and that it is the heart that should become the shrine of God." Turning to the other brahmacharis, She said, "He thinks that externalcleanliness is not very important. 'Didn'tSabari bite into each piece of fruit she offered LordRama in order to make sure that it was ripe and sweet? Didn'tKannappa[4] offer the Lord meat, and flowers which he had been wearing on his own head? He even bathed an image of the Lord with water he carried in his mouth.' He is thinking like this."

The brahmachari turned pale and hung his head. Even though it was done in a lighthearted way, Mother had said exactly what he was thinking. In a few seconds he raised his head and spoke in a tone full of genuine remorse. "Amma, please forgive me," he said. "What you have said just now is absolutely correct. You have understood all my thoughts. Amma, please enlighten me." His eyes were filled with tears.

---

[4] Kannappa was a hunter who came upon a Shiva temple while hunting in the forest. He spontaneously felt loving devotion for the image of Lord Shiva installed there. Though knowing nothing of ritualistic worship, he felt the reality of the Lord's existence in the image and began to worship in his own way. He offered freshly killed boar meat to the Lord, carried water from the river in his own mouth and spit it on the Lord to bathe Him, and carrying flowers in his hair, adorned the Lord with the same. From the orthodox viewpoint, all these actions were a sacrilege trespassing the rules of ritual purity. The priest who was regularly worshipping there would find the meat before the Lord every morning and was infuriated. He finally had a dream wherein the Lord told him that Kannappa was His greatest devotee and that He would prove it the next day. The priest hid in the temple when Kannappa was expected. The next day when Kannappa came for worship, he noticed that one of the Lord's eyes was bleeding. He tried various remedies which all failed to stop the flow of blood. At last he resolved to give his own eye in exchange for the Lord's ailing one. He poked out his eye and placed it over the bleeding one. Then the Lord's other eye began to bleed. He then started to poke out his other eye. Seeing his devotion, the Lord restored his sight and spread his fame.

Although the brahmachari was a bit upset at being exposed in front of everyone, his confession evoked much laughter. Mother became very animated and began laughing like a child. As She kept on laughing, Mother pushed and pulled those who were standing near Her. At one point She caught hold of Balu's long hair and pulled hard. "Ouch!" he shouted, which created another round of laughter.

When the laughter subsided, Mother sat down and continued, "Son, your thinking is correct. But is your mind as pure as Sabari's and Kannappa's were? It is true that Kannappa's and Sabari's behavior was not in keeping with traditional rules; but their hearts were pure. They were as innocent as children. Do you have this kind of purity and innocence? Would you poke out your eyes as Kannappa did? Would you be able to perform such a great sacrifice? Or can you be like Sabari, who waited every day for her Lord with a heart filled with intense longing and love? You can do neither; so what is the meaning of such lofty thoughts?

"It was out of pure and innocent love that Kannappa and Sabari made those offerings to their Lord. When your heart is full of innocent love, you are absent, the ego is absent. In that state, only Love is present; in that state, individuality disappears and you become one with the Lord. You become as innocent as a child. When a child offers something, it cannot be rejected because a child's love is untainted and pure. When you dwell in pure innocent love, there are no dual feelings like pure or impure, good or bad, and so forth. There is only love. Pure love cannot be rejected. When Kannappa and Sabari made their offerings to the Lord, the objects in themselves were not very significant; it was their hearts filled with love that were offered to the Lord. They themselves became the offering. Just like children, so full of love, they transcended even the concept of purity and impurity; they forgot about do's and don'ts.

"Son, when people cannot do something or when they find a certain thing too hard to accomplish, they try to find justification for their own actions. This is human nature. When they realize they are going to lose, they search for a way out. Even if it does not make much sense, theyrationalize. This is a very subtlevasana. This is another trick played by the mind. Be careful and be attentive about this aspect of the mind. A seeker should not fall a prey to such weakmindedness."

The brahmachari who had gone in search of rope returned. Mother stood up and took the rope. With the help of the others in the room, She made a clothesline by tying the ends on two opposing poles of the hut; then She began folding the clothes one by one and putting them on the clothesline. After this Mother walked around and collected all the unnecessary and useless items lying here and there in the room. Some of the things had been inserted in the walls which were made of thatched coconut leaves, and other items were lying in a dark corner of the hut. There were scraps of paper, old clothes, a worn-out toothbrush and an empty toothpaste tube, broken pens, and more. Before throwing each item into an old bucket hastily converted into a trash can, Mother asked the brahmachari who lived in the hut, "Do you want this?" or "Do you have any use for this?" If he said 'no', Mother threw it in the trash can. If he said 'yes', She gave it back to him. This sorting out of the things went on for some time.

Next Mother inspected the *asana* which was spread in front of the altar. It was a thick cloth on which the brahmachari sat for meditation. She smelled it and made a funny face indicating that it smelled bad. Handing the asana to another brahmachari, Mother said, "Wash this for him."

Now everything was in order, and Mother Herself did the final sweeping of the room. One brahmachari lit some incense and Mother sat down on a mat to relax for a while. Gayatri came and offered Mother something to drink. Mother took a single sip and returned the glass to her. Gayatri waited, holding the glass for some time, hoping that Mother would ask for more, but She did not. "Some more, Amma?" Gayatri asked. "No, that is enough," came the reply. Mother asked Gayatri to sit next to Her, then She lay down with Her head resting on Gayatri's lap and sang

Kannunir toratha ravukal

*How many nights have I spent
With my eyes flooded with tears?
O Compassionate One,
Won't You come today?
O Sreedhara Krishna,
During each moment of waiting
I am caught for an eon
In a rain of scorching fire.*

*Throughout each night I wait for You
Believing that the dancing swords of lightning
Are a sign of Your pageantry.
I remain where I am,
Imagining each undertone emerging from the dark
To be the sound of Your footsteps.*

*O Kanna,
Who is eternally free from sorrow,
Whose heart is softened by Love,
When may I see Your gentle smile?
When will You come and save this weeping girl
Drowning in her tears?*

*O Madhava Krishna,
Bless me that I may be reborn*

As a blade of grass
Or a grain of sand on Your path;
Or else, make me a speck of sandalwood paste
To be used by the servants of Your devotees.

After the song Mother remained indrawn for a few moments. When She opened Her eyes, the same brahmachari spoke again, "Amma, by cleaning this room you were actually punishing me." He then corrected himself, "Forgive me, Amma, I shouldn't use the word punish. I know you do not punish anyone. You only correct us in order to teach us to be better. The lessons we receive through your words and deeds are for our own good. You 'punish' us only out of love and compassion. But we are so ignorant that most of the time we forget this. When Mother exposed my thoughts, and while You cleaned my room, and especially when You took my dirty asana and handed it to another brahmachari asking him to wash it for me, I felt terribly ashamed and hurt. I thought Mother was deliberately trying to humiliate me in front of all the others. I know this is not the attitude that a sadhak should have. But, Amma, I feel helpless; these negative tendencies and feelings are so strong." His eyes were filled with tears and his throat was so choked he could not continue.

Mother stroked the brahmachari's forehead and caressed his head with great tenderness and love. "These tears are the impurities within you," She told him. "These tears should be transformed into 'those' tears. These tears come from the pain and anguish caused by the world. But 'those' tears are the tears of bliss which are shed out of pure love and devotion." Mother smiled as She spoke. It seemed that Her smile and eyes held enough power to remove any amount of pain or sorrow. The divine touch of Mother's hand soothed the brahmachari, and the heaviness born out of a guilty conscience continued to stream out in the form of tears. After having wept for some time, he managed to control his tears and soon began to look relaxed and free of mental pain.

Mother's darshan is a healing process, a wonderful divine healing process. Her touch heals the wounds caused by a painful past. Her presence purifies, uplifts, and carries us towards our true Self. Mother is purity embodied. Thus all those who come in contact with Her are transformed and cleansed. In some cases this purification can be seen, while at other times, it is subtle. How many of Mother's devotees are familiar with the seemingly innocent hug that transforms lives, and with the look that causes hearts to melt. Whether you are aware of it or not, whether or not you feel worthy, thispurification happens. Just as an iron piece is magnetized when it is rubbed constantly by a powerful magnet, an ordinary soul is transformed into a spiritual being through the constant contact and companionship of a Mahatma like Mother.

How to handle insults

Now that the brahmachari was feeling better, Mother continued to speak, "Son, there is nothing to worry about. Negative feelings will arise. It is just the past showing up. At least you have confessed your feelings. That means you are not a hypocrite. There are very few people who can remain calm and unhurt when their faults and weaknesses are exposed. These hurt feelings have come up now, in Mother's presence, and the negative feelings will disappear in your love for Her. But in other cases,negativity will remain and can create another deep wound. Be careful about that.

"Negativity after negativity will form a long, long chain attached within you. You have been insulted and scolded numer- ous times in the countless births you have taken. When somebody insults you, he is insulting you from his past, and when you react, you, too, are reacting from the past. Both of you have been victims of insults and have made others your victims in your previous lifetimes as well as in this lifetime. So all your actions and all your words, whether positive or negative, reflect your past. The storing up of the past exists within you. The storage within you is full, overloaded even. To empty the ego which is the sum total of all these negative feelings, one should first of all feel the heaviness of it. Still, it is a wonder that you do not feel the heaviness of the load. If you start feeling the heaviness that is a good sign. From that point on you will start unloading it.

"Amma has heard thestory of a disciple who was instructed by his master in this way: for three years he was to give money to everyone who insulted him, and was not to utter a word back to them. When his period of trial was over, the master said to him, 'Now you can go to the world of true knowledge and learn wisdom.' When the disciple was about to enter the world of true knowledge, he met a wise man who sat at the gate insulting everybody who came and went. This wise man also insulted the disciple, who immediately burst out laughing. 'Why do you laugh when I insult you?' asked the wise man. 'Because,' answered the disciple, 'for three years I have been paying for this kind of thing, and now you give it to me for nothing.' The wise man said to him, 'Enter the kingdom of knowledge; it is all yours.'

"Laugh heartily at those who insult you, seeing their past coming through the words. Reward those who insult you. Try not to utter anything bad to them and slowly, in due course, try not to have any bad feelings against them at all. Act, but do not react. By doing so, you will enter into the deeper realms of your own consciousness.

"Now, when you thought that Amma was insulting you, you could keep quiet and did not react. Furthermore, you confessed that you felt hurt when Amma said those words. This is a good sign. Try the same with others. When others insult you or get angry with you, try to keep your mouth shut, imagining that you are in Amma's presence and that it would be disrespectful to react. Try to feel respect for the other person, because, in truth, he is doing something good for you. He is teaching you to be silent, to be patient. Start feeling pity for him, for his wounded past, feel deep concern and compassion for him. 'Poor man, he is suffering all those deep wounds from the past. He is sick. I should really help him as much as I can.'

"You may still have all the reactions within. You may be boiling within. Yet through proper understanding, penetration, and awareness, try to see that your accuser is suffering from his past wounds. You do not want to hurt a wounded and suffering person. That is cruelty. You do not want to be cruel. You are a sadhak, a seeker; you want to be kind and compassionate.

"It is possible that you may feel respect, but not compassion and concern. Once compassion arises, you forgive the other person. You forget his abusive words. A compassionate person cannot react, for he can only be compassionate. This is difficult to attain in your present mental state, but that is okay. To let go is not so easy. You may fail to feel love. Just as in this situation with Amma, first your silence was out of respect and reverence, or call it fear, for Amma. But still you had a little bit of reaction within. After some time, you contemplated and thought well enough to confess your mental reaction to Amma. Thus if you feel respect for the other person, consider him as a teacher who teaches you patience; or if you can imagine that Amma is talking through him, you will be able to keep silent. It is just like your school teacher scolding you for misbehaving in the classroom or for not studying the lesson properly. You do not shout back at him. You keep quiet out of respect, don't you? Keep silent and move away from the person who insults you. If you remain physically in the presence of a person who is abusing you, you may eventually react even though you had succeeded in keeping your mouth shut in the beginning. Therefore, physically move away from that kind of atmosphere.

"Or, if you must stay, try to recall some fond memories, such as the most unforgettable events you had with your spiritual master, the day you met him, how he showered his love and compassion upon you. Recalling uplifting ideas and cherishing sweet memories can help you keep silent.

"Yet, even though you are able to remain silent while he utters words or retorts, you may still have thoughts of hatred and revenge towards him for his mean and abusive behavior. But you must also be careful not to have any revengeful feelings towards the person. Do not carry the wound of anger and hatred in your mind. Remember that he wanted to teach you something; he had a message for you. You should have an ear and a heart to hear the message and absorb it. You will have to work on acceptance of this later. Meditate, pray, chant, repeat your mantra, and contemplate deeply to remove those and other emotional disturbances."

Chapter 5

An unforgettable boat journey

Friday, 7 September, 1984

In the evening Mother went to visit the house of a devotee in a nearby village. As his house was situated several kilometers away from the Ashram, Mother decided to travel there by boat. Soon after the evening bhajans ended, Unni, who lived just in front of the Ashram, was ready with the boat. The group traveling to the devotee's house consisted of Mother, Gayatri, Damayanti (Amma's mother), Harshan (Amma's cousin), Satheesh (Amma's brother), Balu, Rao and Sreekumar. By eight-thirty in the evening the party set off on the journey with Unni as the boatman.

As they sailed on the backwaters, the reflection of the moon on the water created a play of light and shade. All of nature was bathed in moonlight. The vastness and expansiveness of the sky above had a very soothing effect on the mind. A gentle breeze added to the feeling of calmness. Mother's gaze was fixed on the peaceful sky. Sitting in the boat, She looked extraordinarily beautiful in the moonlight.

A few moments later, as if She were talking to the moon, to the sky, to the infinitude or to something of which no one could know, Mother pointed Her index finger up towards something indefinite. Remaining in this position for some time, Mother began singing. All the passengers responded with vigor, enthusiasm and joy

Adiyil parameswariye

O Supreme Goddess,
Mother of the Universe,
You are my only goal in this world.

O Mother, with beautiful eyes
Like the petals of a blue lotus,
You are the Sustainer of the three worlds,
The One who dwells
within the flower of Maya.
O Beautiful One, the Source of everything,
Rid me of all sorrows.

O Gracious One, Destroyer of greed,
Who leads us through the land of transmigration,
Protect me.
O Mother, giver of devotion and liberation,
O Katyayani, far-famed One, I bow to You.

O Goddess of the earth,
Who is Wisdom and Knowledge,
You are the only delight and the only nourishment;
You are all of Creation.
O fulfiller of all desires,
Please rid me of my pride
Dwell within my mind and remove my distress.

Throughout the song, Mother was looking up at the cloudless sky. She sang another song and in the middle of it went into samadhi. With both Her arms outstretched as if supplicating the Supreme Being, Mother remained motionless for some time. Her eyes were open, but they were transfixed. The unearthly glow on Mother's countenance was made even more radiantly beautiful by a beaming smile which adorned Her face. She shone like another moon.

Mother's divine mood continued for several minutes. Later when She was Her normal self again, Mother noticed two of the brahmacharis talking to each other. Mother said to them, "Children, talking unnecessarily is one of the greatest enemies of asadhak. This opportunity to travel so intimately with Mother is rare. You may not get another chance to spend time with Amma like this. Look how beautiful the night is. Look at the vast, expansive sky and the beautiful moon shining among the glimmering stars. Feel the calmness and silence. Feel the gentle breeze that blows so sweetly and see the trees and bushes on either side of the backwaters. Listen to the *pranava mantra* reverberating from the ocean. Look at the dark blue waters and enjoy the beauty of Nature with the awareness that these are all expressions of the Divine.

"Amma never used to sleep at night. In the early days She would stay awake and call out to the Lord. She cried, prayed, meditated, and danced in bliss. Moonlit nights were Amma's favorite times. On those silent and peaceful nights Amma would become totally oblivious of everything around Her. Her longing for the Divine would reach its peak. She would spend the entire night seeing everything as an expression of the Supreme Absolute, crying and praying and dancing in bliss.

"Sadhaks love the night. That's when they can dive deep into their own consciousness. In the beginning stages it is good for one's spiritual progress tomeditate and pray during the night, especially after midnight when the entire world goes to sleep. It's the best time for a sadhak to stay awake and do hisspiritual practices. In more advanced stages he will be able to meditate and pray anytime he wants, regardless of time or place. When he is able to meditate with such focus, both day and night will come under his control. But that is possible only when his mind becomes so completely fixed on the object of meditation that he doesn't care when or where he meditates. Wherever it may be, he simply gets absorbed in a meditative mood. But before a sadhak reaches this state of spontaneous meditation, he should select ideal conditions for meditation.

"Therefore, children, do not waste these opportunities by talking about silly things. Utilize the time for meditation, silent prayer, and repeating your mantra. Look at the sky and try to visualize the form of your beloved deity there. Try to imagine that He or She is moving with you. Try to see yourIshta Devata's face in the moon or imagine that the moon is the face of the Divine Mother or of Krishna or Rama. As the wind blows try to feel that it is the gentle caress of your beloved deity. Look into the water and visualize the smiling face of your Ishta Devata there. You can imagine that your beloved deity is calling you near, hugging you, kissing you, caressing you, blessing you, and then hiding in the clouds and coming out again a little later. By this kind of imagination you go deeper and deeper into your own consciousness. You enshrine His or Her form within your heart. You open up more and more, and you get closer and closer to your own Self."

Mother stopped and asked everyone to meditate, repeat their mantra, or to imagine that they were merging with infinity as they looked up at the sky. Mother sat silently looking at the sky. The boat kept on moving slowly. The only sound was the rippling of the waters as the boat gracefully glided upstream. This period of meditation and silent prayer continued for half an hour. Even afterwards there was not much talking. Mother sang

Mara yadukula hridayeswara

O most charming One,
Lord of the Yadavas' hearts,
Who is the color of a rain cloud,
Who bears the Goddess Lakshmi on Your breast;
O lotus-eyed One,
Where are Your gentle fingers
That caress the lullabies to sleep?

O You who lived in Vrindavan as Nanda's son,
Who danced and played in the heart of Lord Chaitanya,
And in the hearts of others;
You are bound to Your devotees;
You are the beginning and the end of everything.
We join our palms in adoration to You.

Mother's blissful singing deepened the silence. The hallowed mood went straight into everyone's heart. Mother's presence in the boat remained the very source, the heart and soul of these inspiring moments. In that peaceful and serene atmosphere Mother chanted Her favorite mantra, 'Shiva... Shiva... Shiva... Shiva...' Every now and then Her soft and gentle utterance of the mantra helped everyone remain at the center of his consciousness, even though the natural tendency was to let the mind drift.

After an hour and fifteen minutes, the party reached the devotee's house. Even when the boat stopped in front of the house, which was situated on the banks of the backwaters, nobody felt like getting out or even saying a word. The bliss and peace which Mother radiated permeated the air to such an extent that no one wanted to spoil this precious moment by engaging in any unnecessary conversation. Seeing everyone still sitting in the boat, Mother said, "Hey children, what happened? Are you all in samadhi?" Mother's words awoke them from their indrawn state, and everyone quickly got out of the boat.

Rejoicing at the sight of Mother and Her brahmacharis, the family ushered them to the front entrance where together the husband, wife and children ceremonially washed Mother's feet. Their youngest daughter garlanded Mother, and the father and mother together waved the camphor flame in front of Her, performing the *arati*. The family members then sipped the sacred water from the *pada puja* and sprinkled it on themselves and everywhere in the house. They all offered their prostrations to Mother, who expressed Her love and compassion to each one of them in Her natural, innocent way.

The evening began with the *Lalita Sahasranama,* the chanting of the Thousand Names of the Divine Mother, and continued with devotional singing. Mother Herself performed the arati, the concluding ceremony of waving the camphor flame in front of the images on the altar. This closing worship and chanting of prayers created a serene atmosphere in the house, but above all, Mother's divine presence made the entire event perfect and heavenly.

Midnight came quickly and everyone had a late supper. Mother ate only a few spoonfuls of one of the side dishes and had a few sips of plain water. The family members wanted Mother to eat more, but Mother refused in a loving way. The woman of the house complained sadly, "Maybe it is because of our lack of devotion that Amma is not eating anything from our house." Mother most affectionately but emphatically said, "No, daughter, not at all. You know Amma's nature; She is unpredictable. Amma does not feel hungry, and it is very late. You have already fed Amma with your love; Amma is full with that."

Nevertheless, Mother let the wife feed Her with a piece of *dosa*, a pancake made with rice flour. As she fed Mother with the attitude of a mother feeding Her child, the woman seemed full of affection and joy. Perhaps it was because of the woman's innocent love that Mother spontaneously opened Her mouth again until finally the third time Mother closed Her mouth and said, "Enough, daughter." The woman was ecstatic. She kissed Mother's cheeks and distributed the remaining portion of the dosa as prasad to everyone.

After supper Mother came out of the rather small house which was no more than a hut thatched with coconut leaves. The family had remarked about the small size of their house to which Mother replied, "Children, your hearts are big enough." The front yard was spread with milky white sand, and from the front yard one could step right into the backwaters where the boat was moored. As Mother sat in the sand near the backwaters, she was surrounded by the family members, the brahmacharis, Damayanti, Unni, and Satheesh.

The youngest daughter came and sat on her mother's lap. The girl's mother said to the brahmacharis, "It is this child who was saved by Mother. And for that we have become eternally grateful and devoted to Mother. We all thought that our daughter would not live very long. This little one had chronic asthma. We tried all kinds of medicines but they were of no use. We were utterly helpless, so as a last resort we went to Ammachi. She gave the girl some sacred water. After blessing some more water, Mother told us to give her a sip or two everyday. Mother also instructed us to rub the sacred ash on her chest. That was all we did and the asthma never returned. Now the girl is perfectly healthy."

Mother did not pay much attention to the woman's narration. Mother asked the child, "Don't you feel sleepy?" The girl shook her head and said, "How can I when Ammachi is here!" "You clever, mischievous little girl," Mother remarked with a big smile. Then She asked one of the brahmacharis to sing a *kirtan*

Mauna ghanamritam

In the abode of impenetrable Silence
Of eternal Beauty and Peace,
Where the mind of Gautama Buddha was dissolved,
In the Effulgence that destroys all bonds,
On the Shore of Bliss
Which lies beyond the reach of thought.

In the Knowledge that bestows eternal harmony,
The Abode without beginning or end,
The Bliss known only when
The movements of the mind subside,
At the Seat of Power,
The Region of perfect Consciousness.

At the Goal that bestows the sweet state
Of eternal non-duality
Described as 'Thou art That,'
That is the place where I long to reach;
But I can only do so
Through Your Grace.

When the song ended, Mother asked them to sing another one. It seemed that Mother wished to avoid conversation for a while. When the second song was over, Mother said, "One more." After the third song, Mother sat silently looking at the dark blue sky. Ten or fifteen minutes passed in silence. Suddenly there came the sound of an engine as the daily passenger ferry boat with its puttering engine passed by the house. Pointing to the big motorboat, Mother said, "Amma used to travel in such a boat when She was sent to work in relatives' houses. While traveling in the boat, Amma used to hum '*Omkara*' (the sacred syllable OM), or She would chant kirtans to the rhythm of the engine. Traveling in a boat was a highly spiritual experience for Amma. Constantly remembering the form of Her beloved deity, Amma used to sing, pray, repeat the mantra, and meditate on such occasions. She would not waste even a single moment."

One of the brahmacharis commented, "Amma, it was so effortless and spontaneous for you to get into that divine mood, because that is your nature. But how can we, who are still in the physical and mental bodies and in the grip of vasanas and thoughts, get into that mood? How can we even think of attaining that without your Grace?"

Mother replied, "Children, if a person really wishes to do something, he can do it. This feeling, 'I am weak; it's too difficult; it's impossible for a person like me to reach there,' is not fit for a spiritual seeker. He should believe that he has this power within him and that he can reach it. Each one of you has the beauty and power of a saint or a sage. Each one of you is an infinite source of power. Yet when you see a saint or a sage, or a powerful person, you recoil, saying, 'No, this is for those special people. I can't do it. I have my own tiny little world to bother about, and that's enough for me. Divinity is none of my business, so I'm not going to poke my nose into it.' This kind of an attitude will never help you to come out of the small, hard shell of your little ego. This weakness makes man helpless and inactive. That is why Vedanta tells us to contemplate the Vedic dictum, 'I am Brahman. I am God. I am the Universe. I am Absolute Power, the totality of consciousness which makes everything beautiful and shiny, full of life and light.'

"Self-deprecating thoughts are not good for a sadhak. Such thoughts are not good even for a person living in the world. God has blessed us all with this precious gift of human birth. We have a well-developed body, mind, and intellect. We can learn or do whatever we want. It is only a question of utilizing the instruments or faculties given by God for whatever we choose to pursue. If one chooses the path of spirituality, one is not supposed to remain idle waiting for Grace to come. Realization does not just come automatically; there is great work involved. Realization cannot be purchased. It is not like going to the ice cream parlor and buying an ice cream cone. Even that involves work. How was the ice cream made? It doesn't just materialize out of thin air. Where did you get the money to buy it? It is hard-earned money, isn't it? Suppose there is ice cream at the shop and you have the money, but you don't buy it. It's simple, you won't eat ice cream, will you? Yet you have an intense desire to eat ice cream. So you lie in bed and think of eating chocolate ice cream. You daydream about the different flavors, and you dream about eating and enjoying ice cream, but still you haven't actually eaten any. It is not that there was no ice cream; there are all sorts of flavors available. You have the money and you can obtain as much as you want, but you don't feel like getting up and going to the ice cream parlor. You only think about it and dream about it.

"In a similar manner God is there, the Guru is there, and Grace is always there. You have all the faculties to know and experience this. You have a map and have been given the directions in the form of the Guru's words. The wind of his Grace is always blowing. The river of his divine being is always flowing, and the sun of his knowledge is always shining. He has done his part. His work was over long, long ago.

"Yet, you think the Guru has not done anything. You think that he is not letting his Grace flow. You think that you do not have his blessing or Grace, so you are still waiting for him to bestow it upon you without doing anything yourself. You wait for the day, for the moment, when he will touch your heart. It is all right to wait, but are you really waiting with faith and one-pointedness like the Gopis of Vrindavan, or Sabari, Sri Rama's great devotee? No, you aren't. You might be waiting, but your whole being is not waiting. You are not burning with love and devotion. While waiting you are engaged elsewhere. Your mind is chasing a thousand other things. You are not waiting solely for His Grace. Instead, you are waiting for numerous other 'important things' to happen in your life, and along with those, you also want Grace to happen. And you want Grace to happen for free.

"You may be waiting for God or God's Grace, but the thought of God occurs in you only once in a blue moon, or on Sundays, or at best two or three times a day. Furthermore, those few occasions on which you may think of God are very dull and lacking in intensity, because you are preoccupied with so many other supposedly important things. It is all right if you faithfully wait for Him to come, but be sure you are attentive in your waiting. If you are preoccupied with other things, how can God come? How can His Grace flow? The Guru is there. His ever-flowing Grace is there; it is always present. But you want Him to come uninvited, without any effort on your part. In the name of waiting you idle away your time. You do not consider it an intrinsic part of your life to wait faithfully. You do not take this period of waiting seriously and sincerely. You say, 'I am waiting for God, for His Grace to come. He is all-compassionate, so He will come. Until then, let me engage in other important matters.' This is foolishness. You will neither receive Grace nor will you have the power to overcome difficult situations with this kind of faith.

"It is possible to become the master of the entire universe. You have that potential within you, but you must work. Actually, you are already the Lord of the universe. You are the emperor of the entire world, but you are dreaming that you are a beggar who has to beg for food. The moment you stop dreaming, the moment you realize that the present so-called waking state is, in fact, a dream, you will realize that you are the Lord of the universe, and you will awaken to God-consciousness.

"The whole world, each object in this universe–the sun, the moon, the stars, the galaxies, the milky way, the earth, the mountains, the valleys, the rivers, the ocean, the trees, the animals, the birds, the plants, the flowers, and the entire human mind, all minds–are under your control. You are the master of everything. The entire universe is waiting to welcome and accept you as Lord. But you are still begging with a bowl in your hand. Open your eyes and try to see clearly. You are a king disguised as a beggar. Throw away the beggar's clothes. The universe is waiting for you to don an emperor's robes. Come out of this dream, this illusion of weakness.

"Amma has heard a story about a student who was taking an examination. The question had to do with writing an essay on the religious and spiritual significance of the miracle of Christ's turning water into wine. The students in the examination hall were writing furiously for two hours, filling their exam booklet with their ideas of what the miracle meant. Towards the end of the allotted time, the proctor discovered that one student had not written anything, not a single word. The proctor insisted that he write something before turning in his exam booklet. The student picked up his pen in his hand and wrote, 'The water met its master, and blushed.'

"Children, everything is within you. You are the master of all the five elements. By your mere look, or touch, they will become what you wish. Therefore, do not think, 'O Amma, it happened to you and to you alone. It could not happen to me with all my vasanas and weaknesses. It cannot happen to me. So I will wait till you shower your Grace for this to happen.'

"Do not think that God will enter uninvited. He is already an uninvited guest everywhere, in every nook and cranny of the world, in every inch of space. There is not even a gap between atoms where He isn't. Everywhere in this world He is an uninvited guest. But you will have to recognize Him."

God the uninvited guest

The brahmachari asked, "I don't understand. You said God will not come uninvited, but you also say that He is an uninvited guest everywhere in this universe. This seems to be a contradiction."

Mother responded, "Children, God iscompassion. He is waiting at the door of every heart. He is an uninvited guest everywhere because whether you call Him or not He is there. Whether you are a believer or a non-believer, He is within you uninvited. Behind every form, behind everything, God is hiding. He beautifies things and makes them what they are. He is the hidden formula of life. But He won't reveal Himself to you. You won't feel Him unless you call Him. Prayer is the invitation. You must invoke Him throughprayer andmeditation. Chanting, singing and repeating the mantra are invitations, asking God to reveal Himself.

"You should have the ability and power to recognize God, the God in everything and in every being. This is not possible unless you see the God within yourself. Once you know godliness, which is your real nature, you will know godliness in others. Then you will see God seated everywhere, uninvited.

"Children, God cannot break in. He is not aggressive, because He is love. God is not a person; He is Consciousness. He cannot break in, because Consciousness cannot be aggressive. Invite Him and He will step in. But even uninvited He is waiting there at the door, waiting to be called in. The uninvited God remains hidden outside your heart. He is ever-present, waiting with love and compassion. His glory and splendor are ever-present yet hidden, because you have not invoked the power of His presence through prayer and meditation. Through your invitation, through your prayers and meditation, God will step into your heart and reveal His presence. Then you will know that He was always there waiting for you to call Him."

Everybody listened attentively to Mother's inspiring words. The time was now two o'clock in the morning. No one was at all sleepy, not even the youngest child of the family, who was still sitting on her mother's lap, gazing at Mother's face. The girl's mother said, "Look at this girl. She usually can't stay awake past nine, but today She's wide awake even after two o'clock in the morning." Mother looked at the girl and asked, "Daughter, don't you want to go to bed? Aren't you tired?" The girl shook her head.

Everyone continued to sit in silence, watching Mother as She sat gazing beyond the night sky. Then She raised Her hand up towards the sky and began to sing

En manasin oru maunam

I am dejected because Sri Krishna hasn't come;
I have not yet seen Him,
And the longing of my heart
Brings forth a flood of tears.

Is it because He has not yet returned
From grazing the cattle?
Or has He not yet woken up?
Has the dark-colored One forgotten
That my heart is weeping with longing for Him?

Perhaps he has not yet had his milk and butter?
Perhaps His tender feet have slipped somewhere
And He has fallen?
Or are His devotees swarming around Him like bees,
Drinking the honey from His Feet?

O Kannan, why have You not come today?
O You, who are the color of a rain cloud,
Have You forgotten me?
O, please appear before these tear-filled eyes!

After the song Mother sat in a meditative mood. Ten or fifteen minutes passed before She got up. As everyone else arose, Mother said, "Where isHarshan? He is not here." Everybody looked around, but Harshan was not to be seen. In fact, no one remembered having seen him since they reached the house. Usually he would not miss an occasion like this. He would be present throughout, gesturing and cracking jokes. But today he had been very silent during the entire journey. As everyone began to disperse, Mother wandered away from the rest of the group.

Suddenly the quiet night was interrupted by shouting and the sound of coughing and spitting. Everybody ran to the southwest corner of the house, and there they found Mother with Harshan. Earlier in the evening, as everybody had gotten out of the boat, Harshan fallen gone to sleep lying on the bare sand. That was why he did not appear at the puja, the bhajan or the meal. Mother probably surmised that he had gone off somewhere to sleep, so when She got up from the banks of the backwaters, She went looking for him and found him sleeping around the corner of the house with his mouth wide-open. Mischievously, Mother had stuffed his mouth full of sand. Now, as Harshan was coughing and spitting, She was laughing excitedly and enjoying the scene like a child.

Mother's was in a playful mood. She laughed and laughed, and through Her mirth She teased Harshan, "You were sleeping comfortably while everybody prayed and meditated. Happiness must be followed by sorrow. You enjoyed and now you must pay for it!" Harshan had no complaints since he was quite familiar with Mother's different moods. He always enjoyed Her practical jokes, even those played at his expense. Once all the laughter had subsided and Harshan had stopped cleaning out his mouth, the return journey began. It was three-thirty in the morning.

An hour later Mother and Her party had traveled only halfway home to the Ashram. Unni continued to row the boat. Damayanti and Harshan were fast asleep on a mat spread on the floor of the boat. The moon shone richly in the sky as if overflowing with the bliss of Mother's divine presence. The clouds floating up in the sky seemed to dance ecstatically. The trees and plants on both sides of the backwaters waved their leaves and branches in yet another dance as if celebrating a great occasion. Silence and a meditative mood prevailed. Mother seemed to be reveling in Her own solitary world; She remained still, fixing Her gaze at the sky above. The brahmacharis and Gayatri sat looking at Mother's face, drinking in the eternal beauty that She radiated.

The silent, meditative atmosphere lasted for some time. Mother saw Harshan and Damayanti sleeping and said, "It is cool. (Turning to Gayatri) Do you have something to cover them?" Gayatri searched in the bag and took out a shawl. Mother covered Damayanti with the shawl and took the upper cloth of one of the brahmacharis to cover Harshan. Then She returned to Her seat.

The early light of dawn slowly started creeping over the backwaters. Perching on the branches of the trees and flying around in delight, the birds seemed to be chanting their morning mantras. The beautiful sound created a joyous atmosphere. Facing east, Mother sat enjoying the pristine beauty of the dawn. Every now and then Mother burst into ecstatic laughter. Sometimes it was just the sound, "Ho, ho, ho," as if She were greatly excited. In that exalted mood of spiritual union, Mother sat with Her arms stretched upwards. Her face glowed with ecstasy and bliss. Her sudden bursts of laughter created a heavenly rhythm in the silence of the dawn's golden rays. Captivated by the beauty of Mother's mood, Unni stopped rowing and let the boat drift for some time. A large motorboat passed by creating waves on the surface of the backwaters. The little boat with the passengers from the Ashram bobbed up and down, but Unni immediately awoke from his reverie and controlled it with great skill.

Mother spontaneously burst into song

Bhramarame

O hummingbird of my mind,
You are wandering about exhausted
In your search of pure Nectar.
There is a grove of flowering trees
Where there is no sorrow;
It is blissfully nestled
On the bank of the river of devotion.
O mind, do not despair,
For one day Mother will come
To the one who is pure at heart.

O Shakti,
For those who are wise,
You are the Spring of intelligence;
And through the art of Knowledge
You remove all sorrow.
I offer all of my suffering to You
In Whom everything exists.

O Mother, when will You come?
O Mother, don't wait
Until all my energy is dissipated!
Won't You shower Your Grace upon me?
Who else is there but You?
You are my only support.

The song created waves of spiritual bliss and supreme love in the atmosphere of dawn. Like a beautifully carved marble statue, Mother remained still and silent until the boat reached the Ashram shortly after five-thirty in the morning.

Chapter 6

Contentment

Saturday, 8 September, 1984

The weather was clear and the air was crisp and bright. It was around nine-thirty in the morning as the residents and some visiting devotees gathered around Mother in front of the temple. The morning puja had been completed and people were sitting, just enjoying Mother's presence. One devotee took this opportunity to ask a question. "Amma, why does Amma place so much importance on the path ofdevotion?"

"Children," She began, "there are many reasons why we should consider the path of devotion the most suitable path for most people. First of all, it gives muchcontentment to the practitioner. A contented person will have enthusiasm and vigor. He will be very optimistic and endowed with an adventurous mind. His attitude is that life and everything that happens in life is a gift, and this gives him immense patience and strength. Unlike those who pursue other paths, he does not believe that happiness is a right to which he is entitled. As far as he is concerned, there are no rights, there are only gifts. This attitude helps him to accept everything as a gift, both good and bad, and also instills him with courage and faith. Such a person will have a loving and compassionate heart, a child-like innocence, and a pleasing nature. Not wanting to injure anyone or hurt anybody's feelings, he cannot harm anyone. He will also have the power to renounce his comforts and pleasures for the happiness and peace of others. He will experience the same problems in life as everyone else, but he will have the mental ability and balance to remain calm and quiet when adversity arises. He practices acceptance, for his attitude is that life and everything that happens in life is a gift, not a right.

"Such a person derives his power to be content and relaxed from his unshakablefaith in, and love towards, the Supreme Power. And he will have a name and form for this Supreme Power. He may call it Krishna, or he may call it Christ or Buddha. The power of the name that he chants, and the mental image of the form he cherishes, as well as his faith that his Lord is always with him and protects him from all dangers, helps him to be content, relaxed, optimistic and cheerful at all times and in all circumstances.

"Take, for example, the Gopas andGopis of Vrindavan. They were always blissful and happy, full of vigor and cheer. All the work they did carried a special charm and beauty of its own. They were always in a festive mood, and one could see only happy and contented faces all around, for their lives were sparkling with joy. Life was a festival for them, and idleness was non-existent as they sang and danced with great joy while performing any work. Even their customary chores of taking the cows to the meadows, milking them, and selling the milk and butter became blissful work. They had extraordinary strength and courage, and if they had problems, they confronted them most courageously. Always adventurous and loving in nature, they lived life to its fullest.

"What was the source of their contentment and joy? Their faith in their beloved LordKrishna. It was their faith in His omnipotence and their adoration of Him that helped them celebrate all of life. They became fearless and courageous in His presence. So, children, love and devotion for God is the way to contentment. That alone is the way to peace, happiness, courage and fearlessness. Such qualities that help bring us the fullness of life are not easily available to people who practice other paths.

"Look atHanuman, the great devotee of Lord SriRama. He stands as a magnificent example of tireless work, inexhaustible energy and a being of great achievements. There was not a single incident when Hanuman said 'no' to anything he was asked to do. Obstacles were nothing to him. Whenever Rama was struck with a tragic incident, Hanuman was by His side to carry out His commands. Even the seemingly impossible became possible through Hanuman's constant effort, determination and unshakable faith. He was the embodiment of strength, courage, vigor, fearlessness, determination, optimism, discrimination and contentment. Yet he remained Sri Rama's simple and humble devotee, completely surrendered at the Feet of his Lord.

"Contentment ensues fromegolessness. And egolessness comes from devotion, love, and uttersurrender to the Supreme Lord. Egoistic people cannot be content or happy. They are tense because they have fear, and this fear makes them almost crazy. Most of the time such people are hungry for power, and that craving makes them blind. They want to grab and possess everything, not caring if they use mean and wicked ways, not caring if they ruin other people. The constant fear that they will be deprived of their power and possessions haunts them, and increases their fear and discontent. Look at all the dictators of the world. They are the most egotistic people. Craving power and position, they are war-mongers with no concern for the peace and happiness of society. They don't even care about their own wives and children. They are concerned only about themselves and what will happen to them tomorrow and in the future. They have no qualms about what evil means they may use to gain power. Tense with their own discontentment, they carrynegativity around with them and spread it to others. Thus everyone, every single soul around them, is made unhappy and discontent.

"Hiranyakasipu,Prahlada's father, was a typical example of someone who abused power. Children, by looking at his life, you will get a very good picture of how an extremely egotistic person is totally lacking in compassion. Such a person is full of discontent, anger, fear and cruelty. Hiranyakasipu even tried to kill Prahlada,[5] his son, just to protect his own power, name and fame. But look at Prahlada. In all adversities, he was calm and unmoved like a mountain. He was fearless, courageous, and always content. Why? Because he was a true devotee of God. His joy didn't leave him even when he was thrown into the ocean or was condemned to death by being trampled by a mad elephant or burned alive. Through all of this he remained calm and unperturbed. He was content with whatever happened, good or bad, because he considered life and everything that happened in life as a gift from God. All true devotees have this attitude.

"Contentment comes only when you are surrendered, only when you have the attitude of complete acceptance. It arises only when you can welcome impartially every experience in life. You can be fully content when you can smile at and even welcome death. And even if surrender does not happen immediately, one must at least have the willingness to surrender to the Supreme Will. Only then will one be able to enter into that state of everlasting contentment. If one develops this attitude of acceptance, the moment will eventually come when one becomes eternally

---

[5] Prahlada was the son of Hiranyakashipu, king of the demons. Though born in the demon race, he was by nature devoted to God and an abode of all saintly qualities. Hiranyakashipu looked upon Lord Vishnu as his greatest enemy. When he saw that his son was devoted to the Lord, he began to persecute him and finally tried to kill him. All his efforts were unsuccessful, for Prahlada was completely surrendered to Lord Vishnu and was protected by Him. At last, the Lord killed Hiranyakashipu and making Prahlada the king, blessed him with Self-Realization.

content. Do not idle away your time in waiting for contentment. Nothing will happen. Discontent will prevail in a person who waits without doing anything. Prepare your mind and try to develop the willingness to accept and surrender. Try to welcome and receive both the good and bad. Try to build up an attitude that allows you to smile even at death. This is the way to contentment."

Humility and renunciation

A listener commented, "Amma, your explanation is so enlightening. Yet contrary to your statement,Ravana, who was a devotee of Lord Shiva, remained discontent and tense almost all his life. There are also believers who lead discontented lives."

To this Mother said, "Children, it is true that Ravana was a devotee of Lord Shiva, but his devotion was only a means to increase his material power. The spiritual aspect was totally missing in him. In other words, he had no renunciation. He was intensely desirous of accumulating, possessing and enjoying as much as he could. Although he was strong and courageous, he had no love or compassion. Just like any other dictator, he was a power-monger, a person who cared only about himself and his own security. His power, which he derived from the Lord, made him so egotistic and blind that he even tried to lift Mount Kailas, Lord Shiva's abode. Ravana had no humility, no renunciation.

"Withoutrenunciation andhumility one cannot be content. A true devotee has both of these qualities. A person who lacks renunciation and humility can never be content because he still craves material prosperity. His desires are countless and unsatiable. He is never satisfied with what he has. Instead he thinks about accumulating more wealth, more money, a bigger house, a better car, more and more comfort."

"The slogan of an extremely egotistic person is 'more... more... more...' He will always want to replace an object of lower quality

with something of higher quality for his own comfort and satis-
faction. But he will never replace his lower thoughts with noble
ones. The quality of his words and deeds is of no concern to him.
Always fixing his gaze on the future, always trying to figure out
how to do this or that, he will spend his whole life planning,
calculating, and dreaming. Not able to be in the present and
enjoy what is right in front of him, he cannot even relish his food,
because while he is eating lunch he is planning his supper. How
can such a person be happy and content? He cannot. Living the
way he does, he is almost dead; he is like a moving corpse without
the beauty and charm of life.

"The past and future are unreal. They are illusions. The past
is dead and gone. It is not going to come back, and the future
is yet to come. We do not even know whether we will be alive
from one moment to the next. Anything can happen at any time.
Therefore, do not lead an illusory life. Do not fabricate a world
of dreams to live in. You simply cannot live in the future. You
can only live in the present. Thepresent alone is real. Almost all
dictators and skeptics, and those who run crazily after the world
and its pleasures, are living in the future. They never live in the
present, so they cannot be content.

"Ravana was a devotee, but he used God as an agent. His
devotion was only a means to fulfill his monstrous desires. If
he'd had the opportunity, he would even have devoured God.
WhileRama's devotion for God saved society, Ravana's devotion
destroyed it.

"Children, you say that there are also believers who lead discontented lives. But true believers, those endowed with realfaith,
cannot be discontented. A person whose faith is very shaky will
not be content. His faith is divided; he will have doubts. A man
who has an intense desire for material prosperity cannot feel
content. For such people, devotion to God exists in name only.

Theirdevotion is superficial. It is only skin deep. There is no love in their devotion. For them God is an agent who takes care of their wishes and desires. Their God sits on a golden throne somewhere up in the skies. He is a judgmental and punishing God, a God who loves only those who love Him. They believe that God dislikes those who worship and pray to other deities, to other aspects of the Divine. Ganesh will be angry with them if they worship Krishna, they think. Lord Shiva will punish them if they worship Vishnu instead of Him. They have so many strange beliefs. The God they believe in is inaccessible, inhuman, and unapproachable. He is not pleased with people who do not please Him. He may even curse or punish them. Can you call this devotion? This relationship with God cannot be called devotion. It is a divorce from God, a divorce from your own Self. How can such people ever find peace? They don't see the whole. They see only parts. Their prayers are always filled with petty complaints; they lack any feeling of devotion or love. Their prayers are expressions of their selfishness, greed and hatred."

"Listen to thisstory. Once a sannyasin was invited by a widower to pray for the peace of his wife's soul. The sannyasin began to pray, 'Let everyone be happy; let there be no sorrow; let auspiciousness fill the entire universe; let everyone reach Perfection." The husband who was listening to the prayer became upset. He said to the sannyasin, 'Swami, I thought you were going to pray for my wife's soul, but I haven't heard you utter her name even once.' The swami replied, 'I am sorry, but I can't pray like that. My faith and my Guru have taught me to pray for everyone, for the entire universe. In truth, only by praying for the good of the whole world will the individual be benefited. Only if I pray for everyone, will your wife receive her blessing, only then will her soul find peace. I cannot pray in any other way.' The swami was so adamant about this that the husband had no choice but to yield to his wishes. The husband said, 'All right, you can pray as you like. But can't you at least exclude my neighbor from your prayers?'

"Children, if you water the branches of a tree, the water will be wasted. It is only when the roots are watered that the nourishment will reach the branches and leaves of the tree. Likewise, only when wepray for the uplifting of the entire society will we also be benefited fully. Unfortunately our hearts are closed. We have lost our ability and willingness to share. This is the prevalent attitude among people today. We are only interested in our own gain, in what we can acquire and possess for ourselves."

Another question was raised, "It sounds as if Amma is speaking against the accumulation of wealth. But how can people be expected to give up everything they have worked so hard for during their whole life? How can they live without any expectations? How can people simply give up their egos? It sounds impossible for a normal person living in the world."

"Impossible,impossible!" exclaimed Mother. "Children, all you can say is 'impossible.' You make everything 'impossible,' but there is no such thing as 'impossible.' Remember that you are living in the space age. Man has gone to the moon. The other day one of the western children was telling Amma that in the West people rarely use their hands to do any kind of work. They have machines for almost everything. This Westerner was surprised to see how we spend hours carrying sacks of cement on our heads. It takes us a whole night to move what he said a machine could do in less than an hour.

"In the future people may even have electronic spoons to feed themselves; they won't have to use their hands at all; and yet you keep on saying, 'impossible.' It has become a habit to say that everything is 'impossible'. It is easy to say 'impossible' to anything asked of you. It takes no effort, just a few movements of the tongue. Is anything possible as far as you are concerned? This word 'impossible' is a curse on mankind. Try to remove the curse; work hard, and you will see that nothing is impossible.

"It is true that man cannot live without expectations and without his ego. Amma knows that it is not easy to give up all that one has earned through years of hard work and determination. Amma is simply trying to say that a person should not live in a dream world, but should concentrate more on the present than on the future or the past. You can keep your ego if you want; that's no problem. But don't let it eat you up. A person can make use of his ego to put forth effort in his work, to acquire possessions and to engage in pleasurable activities. That's fine. But he must not be blinded by his ego. He must not go against his own conscience, his own human nature. Let him try to live as a human being and not as an animal.

"Blindness of the eyes is bearable and can be managed to a certain extent. You can still live as a human being. You can still have a loving and compassionate heart. But when you are blinded by theego, you are completely blind. Even if you lose your eyesight, if your heart is full of light and love, it will reflect on your deeds and on your entire being. You can still be a human being radiating the light and love of life. Whereas the blindness carried by the ego pushes you into complete darkness. You can't see or hear anything correctly. What you perceive through your eyes and ears is perverted and you react accordingly. You suffer and you also make others suffer.

"You must have heard of the great devotee,Surdas. He was blind, but his blindness was not a problem, for he was full of love and compassion. Singing the glories of his BelovedKrishna, Surdas led a happy and blissful life. Once Lord Krishna and His consortRadha both appeared before Surdas and restored his eyesight. But after beholding the enchanting beauty of his Lord,

Surdas told Sri Krishna, 'My Lord, now make me blind again, for I do not want to see the world with the same eyes that have beheld Your Divine Form."

All of a sudden, Mother's mood changed. Lifting both hands skyward, She began calling out, "Krishna... Krishna... Krishna..." Her supplication was so powerful that it created waves of supreme love in the still air of the morning. All were filled with longing as they sat gazing intently at Her. Mother's call had culminated in silence. As She sat perfectly still, a glowing smile on Her lips, Mother seemed to be in Krishna Bhava. The presence of divinity danced and sparkled in the morning light. A slight breeze stirred the air and Mother began to sing

Anjana sridhara

O beautiful, sapphire-blue Sridhara,
I salute You with joined palms.
Victory to Krishna, salutations to Him!

O You who are like a beautiful jewel,
O Son of Vasudeva,
Remove all my sorrows.

O Krishna,
Who was born as a Divine Child,
Protect me in every way.

O Cowherd Boy,
Please come running
And play your flute.

Some time passed before one of the brahmacharis reminded Mother about theSurdas story. Mother continued, "You may find it difficult to imbibe the essential message of the story of Surdas, but it remains a truth that people like him existed, who could be fully content even without external eyes. It requires rigorous spiritual practice for the inner eye to be opened. Once that is open, the external eyes are secondary. You may say 'impossible' to this as well, however let's come back to the point in question.

"You don't have to give up everything you've gained through endless work. Keep yourpossessions and have great fun in life. But while you are in society, while you are enjoying being with your family and friends, or while you are at work dealing with business associates, don't let your power and position blind you. Allow yourself to express at least some love and concern when it is necessary.

"Don't let your power and position, your name and reputation, your wealth and possessions make you look down on others. If someone who is badly in need of help approaches you, you should have the capacity to smile warmly at him, to have a compassionate word for him and to listen. Even if you do not give him anything, smile at him and console him with a few loving words. You should be able to tell him, 'Brother, I understand your problems. It is quite obvious that you are having a hard time. I wish I could help you by sharing your sorrow, but unfortunately I am not in a position to do so. Please forgive me.' These words will have a soothing effect on him. They will work like a balm for his aching heart. He will be consoled and think, 'Oh, at least he gave me some comfort with his kind words. It is a great relief to know that good-hearted people like him still exist in the world.' He will have new hope and new enthusiasm. He will not be desperate and depressed. He will not think of committing suicide.

"Suppose you behave harshly to someone in need, speaking in a rude way and not showing any concern or compassion to the suffering man. You threaten him and chase him away. Several others before you may have treated him in the same harsh and loveless way, and now, because of your rude and thoughtless behavior, he might lose heart completely. The accumulation of all these rejections might fill him with disappointment and frustration; he might feel desperate and lose all hope to live. In that state of hopelessness he might even end his life. Who is responsible for his death? Who pushed him to death? You contributed, you and the others who ill-treated him. Your ego, power and position made you blind. They made you a heartless person. Your words and deeds reflected the inner blindness caused by your ego.

"Do not give up your wealth. Do not give up your expectations in life. Have them, but try to be a real human being. Try to feel the suffering of others. You are not a machine or an animal or a demon. You are a human being. You represent the human race. Therefore, try to be loving and compassionate, because those are the signs of an evolved life. Remember, only a human being can develop compassion and only a human being can empathize with others. You might think, 'If he is suffering, it is his karma.' It is none of your business to think about his karma. If it is his karma to suffer, consider it your karma to help him. Only helping others will help you evolve. No other species receives this precious gift from God: the ability to understand and be compassionate. Utilize it. Do not misuse it.

"The ability to grow in love and compassion has almost been forgotten. By not making use of this rare gift, you are rejecting God, going against God and denying His gift. This is the worst thing that can happen to you. If something goes wrong in your work, that can be corrected. Material loss is not irreversible. If, for instance, you lose a huge sum of money, it can be replaced. But if you reject God's gift, that is irreparable. He wants you to use it properly. If you reject it, you are obstructing the flow of His Grace. You are building a dam between Him and you. Your ego is the dam.

"Children, Amma knows that, except for a few who can be counted on our finger tips, human beings are ambitious and filled with desires. For almost everyone who lives in the world, it is impossible to live a life without action and the expectation of the fruit of that action. Still, while living in the world, one can lead a happy and contented life. Man has the power to be content if his energies and capacities are directed through the proper channels."

"How is it possible to close off the past and future and let all the energies flow in thepresent?" one of the brahmacharis asked.

"Listen carefully," Mother said. "Suppose the only child of a couple is suffering from a fatal illness. The doctor says that unless a miracle happens, there is little hope. The medicine which he gives the child may or may not work. The doctor says, 'Pray to the Almighty. He is the only one who can make this medicine work. He is the only one who can save the child.' The father and mother normally have little faith in God; but now, out of desperation, they do as the doctor tells them. With great intensity they both begin to pray. Why? Because there is a serious threat and an urgent need. They are now living in the moment. They look at their son. They watch his face and feel his breath. They caress his tiny limbs, and anxiously wait for him to open his eyes. When they see that there is no sign of improvement, they call out to God and they pray. In order to please God, they read one of the scriptures. They express great love and compassion for everyone who comes to see the child. At that moment, even if their worst enemy should come, they would offer him a chair and they would talk kindly to him. They would do this because now they have no feeling of hatred towards anyone. They don't speak ill of anyone. They have suddenly become very humble and loving. It is as if by really living in the present they have become saintly or enlightened for a short period of time, until the child is saved or dies. But, in either case, the old tendencies will soon return.

"But for now why do they behave like this? How is it possible to forget the past and the future at this particular time? They're not concerned about the argument they had the day before. They have forgotten all about it. Their child's life is in danger, and so they have a common aim which is for him to get well. Thus they are now working together with great love. Maybe for the first time in their lives they can really love each other. They don't feel enmity towards anyone. Confronted with the crisis at hand, they do not think about the future. Tomorrow, or even the next moment, does not exist for them. It is impossible for them to think about the future as they sit, full of hope, looking at their son's face.

"All their thoughts are in the now. Will he open his eyes now? Each movement of the child's body fills them with hope. They are in the moment, present to what is at hand, not wanting to think of the possibility of their son's death. They want only to think of life. Because of their common concern for their son, they are in accord with each other, grateful for each other's company and for those who come to visit.

"Where do they get this power to be humble, friendly and loving even to people they don't usually like? How do they get this power to live in the present, to forget the past and the future? Where do they get this great power ofconcentration? They get it from living in the present, living from moment-to-moment with their son's life hanging on the edge of death. An ever-present need and urge helps them live in the present. The threat to their son's life helps them to pray, to be compassionate and friendly towards all who come. They feel that the child needs not only God's Grace but also everyone's blessing and prayer, so they ask the people who come to see him, 'Please pray for him. Please pray for our son.'

"This is just an example to show you that you have the mental power and strength to channel all your energies into the present, forgetting all regrets about the past and anxieties about the future.

"Remember, at each and every moment, this great threat of death is present. When we realize that, it is a blow to our ego. If we can feel the immanence of death, it will help us to live in the present. It will help us to be concerned about others. Your energies can be channeled properly only when you realize the need to do so. You must become conscious that you are wasting your abundant energies, and that they ought to be used for greater achievements in life. Once you are aware of the tremendous loss, you know that your energies must be conserved and put to proper use in order to bring about a wonderful gain. You can remain in the same field of work but can become a tremendously inspiring source of power if your energies are properly channeled."

Be content with what you have

Except for the sound of the wind rustling through the coconut trees and the gentle roar of distant waves, all was quiet. Turning Her gaze away from those gathered around Her, Mother began to sing. Looking towards the sky, Mother poured Her heart out as She sang

Hridaya nivasini Amme

O Mother, who dwells in my heart,
Embodiment of affection,
I can utter nothing but Your sacred Names.
O Mother of the world,
Bestow your Grace
That I may tell Your story.
I do not care for worldly pleasures;

I want only to adore You
With pure devotion.

I have carried many burdens,
Lived life after life without knowing You;
But since I have come to You,
I have surrendered all my burdens.
O Mother, apart from You
I cannot see that anything is lasting;
Let me forget myself
And dissolve in the stream of Your Consciousness.

Mother has told me
That Mother and I are not two
We are One;
But I do not yet perceive this.
I just want to stay with Her
And be Her child.
Mother looks after Her children with love and care
And by the mere touch of Her hand
She washes away my sins.

Oh Mother, am I not your child?
Then why is it taking so long?
I feel I am your child
And am counting each moment.
O Mother, what can I do to get closer to You?
Please show me the way.
O Mother, I am nothing
You are all there is
You are everything.

When She had finished singing, Mother again began to speak.
Gazing at the coconut palms silhouetted against the sky and

the distant backwaters, She said, "Look at the beauty ofNature. Living harmoniously with Nature will in itself bring happiness andcontentment."

Br. Rao said, "It is a pity that human beings, supposedly the most evolved creatures on earth, don't understand this truth. It seems that it has become their nature to complain and be dissatisfied."

Mother said, "There was a time when many, many people in the worldwere so unhappy that they all wailed and lamented to God for relief. Every person who was dissatisfied with his own lot in life complained and said he would gladly change places with someone else. God responded to their cries and appeared before them. All the people with grievances assembled before Him in a large valley. God said to them, 'Peace be with you. Having heard your sorrowful wailing, I have come in response to your prayers. Lay down all your troubles and sorrows in front of Me. Any sickness, disability or woe that causes you discomfort or misery, give it up now.'

"Eagerly the people all threw down their burdens, their sorrows and fears on the valley floor. There was such a large heap of woes that the whole valley was filled and a mountain was formed. God then declared, 'In exchange for what you have given up, you may now select from this mountain of woes any burden you prefer.'

"There was a mad scramble as each person snatched a burden of woe that had belonged to someone else, hoping it would be much better than the one he'd had before. The beggar's burden was exchanged for the rich man's, and the childless woman took the burden that had belonged to a woman with many children. This went on for some time until the mountain of woes disappeared. For the moment, everyone felt happy and relieved. God left them and the people returned to their homes.

"But what do you think happened the very next day? The complaints began again, but a hundred times louder and a hundred times worse than they had been before. So again, God came down and stood before the people. Now they all cried out, begging to be given back all their old problems, as they could not bear the new pain and grief they had chosen. God granted their prayer and they all returned to their old lives, satisfied for the moment, but soon to become dissatisfied again." Everyone laughed at this, recognizing themselves in the people of the story.

Mother continued, "Children, learn to becontent with what you have. Don't desire what you don't have or covet what others have. Don't think that someone else's pain is nothing compared to your own, or that you would feel much better if only you were in someone else's shoes. This is not true. Each individual has his own set of problems and worries. You cannot exchange your troubles for someone else's because you would not be able to bear anyone else's pain. The same is true of happiness. You find that your neighbor is happier than you, and pray to God to be like him. Yet once you experience his happiness you realize that you actually prayed for the wrong thing. Your neighbor's happiness and sorrows belong to him. By the same token, your joys and sorrows are yours alone. Realize this truth and be content with what you have. You cannot have more or less than what is intended for you. What you have is what is meant for you."

Another brahmachari commented, "That is why the scriptures also say, 'The next moment does not belong to us. It is not under our control. Therefore, whatever good you want to do, do it now right now. Do not postpone it.' Isn't that right, Amma?"

"The threat ofdeath is the greatest threat to ourego. It is always there; yet, we don't see it," replied Mother. "We don't hear death's soft steps, and that's why we persist in our tendencies and do not want to change our ways. Ignoring the great challenge of death, we do not exercise love and compassion, and we do not feel like sharing the sorrows and sufferings of other people. That is why we are not humble. The most humbling experience, death, is just one step behind us; therefore, do not say 'tomorrow.' Now is the right time to do what needs to be done. Now we should take an oath for a change to happen in our approach to life.

"Children, here is astory. Once a *brahmin* came to the great kingYudhishthira, seeking help to finance his daughter's marriage. Yudhishthira said, 'Revered brahmin, come tomorrow morning; I will give you the necessary funds then.' The poor brahmin left the palace disappointed. He had many things to arrange and had hoped to get the money immediately.

"A few moments later, cymbals began sounding, trumpets blew, and war drums echoed throughout the citadel. This was quite unusual. Normally this kind of jubilation would take place only when the king returned from a victorious battle. Upon hearing all the commotion, Yudhishthira was annoyed since there was no war going on. He sent a messenger to inquire about the noise, and the latter returned saying that the band party was playing atBhima's[6] command. Bhima was immediately summoned and asked to explain. Bhima replied in a very polite way, 'Your majesty, I was only celebrating your victory.' 'My victory?' exclaimed Yudhishthira. 'But there has been no victory!' Bhima said, 'Oh yes, my Lord, there has. You sent that brahmin away, telling him to return tomorrow. This can only mean that you have gained a victory over death, for who can know anything about the next moment, not to mention tomorrow, but one who has conquered death.' The wise Yudhishthira understood the message hidden in Bhima's action. He realized his mistake, confessed it, and felt

---

[6] Bhima is the second eldest of the five Pandava brothers, relatives of Lord Sri Krishna. The Pandavas, fighting on the side of righteousness, defeated their cousins, the Kauravas, who were ever engaged in wicked deeds. Bhima was renowned for his strength.

thankful to Bhima for helping him to open his eyes to the truth. He then summoned the brahmin and gave him more than enough wealth to perform his daughter's marriage ceremony.

"Children, understanding thatdeath can happen at any moment will help us to have real faith and to move towards God. Death will snatch away all that we have. This body which we love and care about so much will not come with us. We cannot take even a needle with us when we die. Understanding this great truth, take refuge at the Supreme Lord's Feet and be content and happy with whatever comes to you."

The last words Mother spoke resounded within each person's heart, "...take refuge at the Supreme Lord's Feet and be content and happy with whatever you are given..." Mother began to sing

Parinamam iyalatta

O Supreme Goddess, unchangeable One,
Bless me and remove my suffering.
Lord Shiva Himself, who burned down Tripura,
Is not He Your husband?
O please, remove the darkness!
Will the full moon visit me this night?
Are You aware of the darkness in my heart?
The days drop by, like petals falling from a flower,
And still, You do not come.

O Mother,
You are what any small child would long for.
Doesn't a huge tree support a tiny creeper?
O Mother, I don't know what to do;
Help this sad and lonely one;
Let me merge in You.

O Mother,
Exhausted in this desert, I drag myself along;
I cannot even crawl to You.
O Goddess of all,
Take pity on my fate and turn towards me
Grant me refuge at your Feet.

The song ended and everybody sat without talking. One of the brahmacharis took this as an opportunity to clarify another doubt. "Amma, it is said that if you try to pursuehappiness, you will miss it.' Why?"

"Because the search for happiness will cause discontent," Mother replied. "Searching is bound to create turbulence within. A turbulent mind is an unhappy mind. Your search for happiness is always in the future. It is never in the present. The present is within. The future is outside. In your anxiety to gain happiness you create hell in your mind. After all, what is the mind? It is the accumulation of all your unhappiness, negativity and discontent. The mind is the ego, and the ego cannot be happy. How can you seek happiness with such a mind? More seeking will only bring more unhappiness. Happiness ensues only when the mind and all its egocentric thoughts disappear. To be happy, you must forget about happiness. To be content, you must forget about contentment. Stop living in the past and future. Stop seeking happiness and you will find that you are no longer unhappy. Stop seeking contentment and you will suddenly become content.

"Pray for a contented mind in all circumstances.Prayer becomes genuine only when you pray for a peaceful and contented mind, no matter what you get.

"LordVishnu once said to his devotee, 'I am tired of your constant petitioning. I will grant you three wishes. After that, I shall not give you anything more.' The devotee was excited to hear this and did not hesitate to make his first wish. He asked for the death of his wife so he could marry a better woman. This was immediately granted.

"But when friends and relatives gathered for the funeral and began to recall all the good qualities of his wife, the devotee realized he had been too hasty. He realized he had been blind to all her virtues. He began to doubt if he would ever find another woman as good as she had been. So when the time came to make his second wish, he asked the Lord to bring her back to life. Now only one wish remained. He was determined not to make a mistake this time, for he would have no chance to correct it. He consulted many sources, and different people suggested that he ask for different things like health and wealth. Some of his friends told him to ask for immortality. But what good was immortality, said others, if he did not have good health? And what's the use of health if he had no money? And how could he enjoy having money if he had no friends?

"Years passed and he still couldn't make up his mind what to ask for: health or wealth, power or love. Finally, he said to the Lord, 'Please tell me what I should ask for.' The Lord chuckled at the man's predicament and said, 'Ask to be content no matter what you are given.'

"Renounce and enjoy. The real fruit, the real happiness, lies within. Learn to be content with that inner experience of happiness. When you eat a banana, you eat only the fruit. You don't eat the peel because it will give you a stomach ache. Similarly, don't allow your wealth, status and reputation to be the very core of your existence. They may seem to provide happiness, but such happiness is transient and riddled with pain. But remember, your real existence lies within."

Another brahmachari asked, "Amma, while talking about contentment, You said that real contentment can arise only when one understands the spiritual aspect of devotion, and only when one has renunciation. What do you mean by that?"

Mother replied, "The word renunciation scares some people. Their attitude is that if contentment can come only through giving up, then it is better not to be content. They wonder how they can lead a contented life without wealth, without a beautiful house, a nice car, a wife or husband, without all the conveniences and comforts of life? Without all these, life would be impossible, it would be hell, they think.

"But do you know anyone whose possessions make them really happy and content? People who look for happiness in life's many conveniences and comforts are the most miserable ones. The more wealth and comforts one has, the more worries and problems one will have. The more one desires, the more one will feel discontent, because desires are endless. The chain of greed and selfishness continues to lengthen. It is an endless chain. A person who is always thinking about accumulating more and more and more cannot be content. This does not mean that in order to be content one should never want to fulfill any desire. That is not the point. The point is that one should learn to be content with what one has. To merely acquire more wealth and to seek honor and status should not be life's sole aim. Plow the field, sow the seeds, take good care of the seedlings, remove the weeds, give water and manure, and then wait patiently. If all this is done well and with an attitude of self-surrender and love, there will be a bountiful harvest. All actions bear fruit. The future is the fruit. But don't worry about the future. Wait patiently, dwelling in the present, performing your actions with concentration and love. Action is the present. Love each action; find bliss in all that you do. That is the most important thing. When you can live in each moment of action, good results must come.

"Only by living in the present can one fully enjoy what one has. This means that you must stop getting anxious about the results of your actions, and stop worrying about things that have been done in the past. Real renunciation is the renunciation of the past and the future. The past is the garbage can where you have dumped all the actions you have performed. It is a storehouse of everything good and bad. The past is a wound. Don't touch it or scratch it. Don't make it bigger. If you scratch the wound - that is, if you delve into your memories - the wound will get infected. Don't do that. Try instead to let it heal. Healing is possible only through faith and love of God. This is possible only in the present. Remember God, chant His name, meditate on His form, and repeat your mantra. That is the best medicine to heal the wound of the past. Take that medicine to forget the past and do not be anxious about the future.

"Real devotion requires renunciation. This is what most so-called devotees lack. Such a devotee constantly broods over the past, or he dreams about the future, building castles in the air. Even while chanting God's name, he is lost in past memories or creating some future dream. Thus, he misses the beauty of chanting God's name. He does not appreciate the divine beauty of his beloved deity or his Guru's compassionate and loving form, and thus misses the Grace as well. His prayers are empty; he never looks into his own heart. He never enjoys the ecstasy of love and devotion. Lacking absorption, his meditations are dry. Because he can renounce neither the past nor the future, he misses the beauty of the present. His actions are not beautiful. His words cannot inspire.

"Living in the present is the spiritual aspect of devotion. The so-called devotee is more concerned about the material aspect of his faith. For him faith in God is a part-time business. His prayers and meditations are not real. He cannot let go. He is so attached that he sometimes even calls out, 'Oh, I cannot forget my memories! They are grabbing me, binding me.' What a pity! Memories cannot bind him. They are inert and lifeless. They have no power of their own. It is he who gives power to them; it is he who grabs at them. If he would just release his grip, he would be free. He philosophizes a lot about renunciation and selflessness, but he is not sincere.

"Amma has heard thisstory:

One man flatly said to another, 'I love the path of renunciation and selfless service.'

The second man said, 'Hey, do you even know what renunciation and selflessness mean?'

The first man replied, 'Yes, I do.'

'Then,' retorted the second, 'if you have two TV's, you should give one to someone who doesn't have any.'

'Oh, yes I can do that,' said the first.

'Okay,' said the second, 'now if you have two cars, one should go to a person who doesn't have any.'

The first replied, 'No problem. Consider it done.'

Amazed at the first man's big-heartedness, the second man continued, 'So, if you had two cows, you would give one away. Right?'

'No! That's not possible!' the first man exclaimed. 'I can't do that!'

The second man was puzzled, 'Why not? It's the same logic, isn't it? If you're willing to give up a TV and a car, why do you hesitate to give away a silly cow?'

The first man explained, 'No, it's not the same logic at all. I don't have two TV's or two cars, but I do have two cows!'"

Everybody laughed at this wonderful illustration of Mother's teaching. Then She went on, "Children, this is the kind of renunciation we have. We make all sorts of excuses, 'If only I had this I would have helped you. If only I had that, I would have given you what you needed.' But when we do have the means to help, we forget all about our promises. We make promises regarding what we do not have, but are never willing to part with what we have."

Chapter 7

Sahasra-seersha purushaha
Sahasra-akshah sahasra-paath
Sa-bhoomim viswatho vrittwa
Atya-tishtah-dhasangulam

"He, the cosmic Lord, thePurusha, with a thousand
heads, a thousand eyes, and a thousand legs, pervades
the whole universe, and beyond."

– Purusha Suktam

Whether big or small, significant or insignificant, nothing escapes
Mother's sight. She sees everything. It is said in the scriptures that
the cosmic Lord, the Purusha, has a thousand heads, a thousand
eyes, and a thousand legs. He is said to pervade the entire universe
and beyond.

In this context, the word 'thousand' denotes the infinite.
One who has realized God or the Infinite, sees as if through an
infinite number of eyes, hears through an infinite number of ears,
and tastes through an infinite number of mouths. One who is
one with Brahman, feels through everything in creation. Such a
person experiences the world through every mind dwelling in all
the three worlds because all are parts of that infinity.

Such a person cannot miss anything that is happening in the
world. His or Her look penetrates into everything. So, Mother's
eye is the cosmic eye. Her mind is the cosmic mind, for Mother

is one with the universe. She is Infinity. In the Bhagavad Gita, referring to the Supreme Purusha, Lord Krishna says, "All heads are His, all eyes are His, all legs are His." The same is true of Mother. Nothing can escape Her sight.

Soon after coming to stay at the Ashram, one of the brahmacharis had an experience which convinced him that Mother knew everything he did. This happened in the beginning of 1982 when one evening a devotee presented the brahmachari with a big packet of biscuits and told him that they were for all the Ashram residents. There were no more than twelve permanent residents at the time, and at first the brahmachari had every intention of sharing the biscuits with his spiritual brothers. But later, while sitting alone in his little hut, he thought, "Nobody knows that the devotee gave these biscuits to me, and now he has gone. I don't have to worry about his telling the others about them. Let me keep them for myself and enjoy them over the next few days." And so, the brahmachari hid the packet of biscuits behind Mother's picture on his altar and covered it with the altar cloth. He thought that this was a good hiding place. His altar was located in a dark corner of the hut and, in any event, why would anyone look around on his altar? The brahmachari then left his hut and continued with his day. Who can predict what will happen in Mother's presence? After the regular evening bhajan, the unpredictable happened.

When the bhajan ended, Mother walked over to the coconut grove. She wandered among the trees for a few minutes and then, for no apparent reason, went straight into the "biscuit thief's" hut. He was sitting outside at the time, but when he saw Mother entering his hut, the brahmachari rushed to his room behind Her. Mother stood in the middle of the room for a few seconds, then suddenly put Her hands behind the picture and pulled out the biscuits. The brahmachari turned pale and stood with his head hung in shame. Soon he fell at Mother's feet and began to weep.

With a mischievous smile on Her face, Mother stood there with the biscuits in Her hands. After some time Mother asked the brahmachari to get up. He stood, but without raising his head. From that position, he begged forgiveness through his tears.

Still glowing with a bewitching and mischievous smile, Mother coolly held the biscuit packet in Her outstretched hand. She didn't show even a wrinkle of consternation as She said, "Son, take these. They are for you. You can eat them all alone. Don't feel bad." Hearing Mother's softly put but sharp words, the brahmachari cried aloud saying, "Amma, please don't torture me anymore!" Now Mother could not hide Her compassionate and loving qualities any longer. She put the brahmachari's head on Her shoulder and consoled him saying, "Son, it was just a joke. Amma knows that you did this out of your childlike innocence. Don't worry. After all, it is Amma who caught you. Don't feel ashamed or hurt. But son, try not to be selfish. If you can't share even a small little thing with your own spiritual brothers, how can you ever share your heart with the entire world? How will you renounce your selfishness, and begin to love and serve the world? This is the place where you have to begin, so try to be more open and sharing."

This incident is just one of countless illustrations of the power of Mother's 'thousands of eyes.' Through it one can see the great beauty and charm in the way Mother points out Her children's mistakes and corrects them. The way She does it cannot hurt, or create a wound. Yet, even if it does create a small wound, Mother knows how to heal it as well. Even though She allows sadhaks to experience a certain amount of pain or tension in order to help them realize their mistakes, the unconditional love and compassion She expresses is so great that it soothes them and heals their pain.

Respect for all life

Friday, 14 September, 1984

A few days ago, one of the residents transplanted a half-grown-mango tree from one spot to another on a plot of land which the Ashram had recently bought. He didn't like the way the mango tree looked where it was, and so, with the help of some other residents, he moved the sapling to a corner of the plot. However, none of them had thought to ask Mother's permission before transplanting the tree.

A day or two after the mango tree had been moved, Mother made an unannounced inspection of the premises. When the brahmacharis saw that Mother was walking in the direction of the new land they looked at each other and started to whisper. They were all afraid because the mango tree had withered away soon after it was moved to a new spot. As soon as Mother reached the new plot, She said, "Something is missing. What is it?" Everyone turned pale; no one spoke. "Shiva! Where is the mango tree!" Mother exclaimed. All remained silent. No one dared to say a word. Mother once again inquired, "What happened to the mango tree? Has someone cut it down?" Finally Br. Pai stepped forward and in a very feeble voice said, "Amma, Nedumudi moved the tree from here to the other side and we all helped him transplant it."

"Where? Where did you plant it?" Mother said in a very worried tone."

With Pai leading the way, Mother and the group walked to the place where the mango tree had been transplanted. Seeing its withered limbs, Mother called-out in a heart-broken tone, "Shivane! What did you do to this tree? How could you do this? What a great sin you have committed. Why didn't you ask me before you moved it? I wouldn't have allowed you to do such a thing. I can't bear the sight of this poor wilted tree."

There was much pain and concern in Mother's words; Her agony was even expressed on Her face. She displayed the feelings and concern of a mother for her hurt child. Mother squatted down on the bare ground with her head down and her hands on her forehead. Those who stood near Mother noticed that She was wiping away tears. While some wondered why Mother would cry over such a silly matter, others were overwhelmed with admiration for the divine love and compassion that She could show towards all of nature, even towards plants. Moved by Mother's emotion, some could not control their own tears.

Moments passed. After a long interval, Mother spoke. "Children, please do not destroy life like this ever again. Such acts are not fitting for those on the spiritual path. Our goal is to feel life everywhere. We should avoid destruction. We have no right to destroy. We cannot create; therefore, we should not destroy. Only God can create, sustain, and destroy. All three are beyond our capacity. Such great feats fall only under His jurisdiction. Therefore, do not repeat such an act. If you cannot judge things and situations properly on your own, seek the advice of someone knowledgeable or wise. And if they cannot give you proper advice, remain still. It is wiser to do nothing than to act foolishly.

"We must remember that everything is sentient, that everything is full of consciousness and life. Everything exists in God. There is no such thing as mere matter; consciousness alone exists. If we approach all situations with this attitude, destruction becomes impossible for us; the very idea of destruction disappears. Only then can you help and serve others for their benefit and for the betterment of the world.

"When Amma talks about the 'world,' She is not talking only about human beings. The 'world' includes everything–humans and animals, plants and trees–the whole of nature. It is true that human beings are the most visibly evolved creatures, but that doesn't mean that other forms of life are without feelings. The *Vedas* and the *Upanishads* say that everything is pervaded with consciousness.

"God dwells in everything. Nowhere is it mentioned that God dwells only in human beings and not in animals or other species of life. He is in the mountains, the rivers, the valleys, the trees. He is in the birds, the clouds, in the stars, the sun and moon, everywhere. God dwells in *sarva charaachara*, in both the moving and the unmoving. How can a person, who has understood this, kill and destroy?

"You may think that humans can speak, walk, act, think and feel, whereas plants cannot; you may think that they are lifeless, and that you therefore have the right to cut them down, destroy them, and use them for your own selfish purposes. However, everything in Nature has a purpose to fulfill. There are no mistakes in creation. Everything in Nature is well calculated and accurately measured. The proportions are perfect.

"Every creature, every thing that has been created by God, is special. Think of the miracles of Nature. Camels are blessed with a special bag to store water; the kangaroo has a cradle to carry its baby wherever it goes; even the most insignificant and seemingly harmful creatures or plants have a specific use. They have a part of their own to play. Amma has heard that spiders keep the insect population in balance; snakes keep the rodent population under control, and even the tiny, one-celled plankton in the ocean serve as food for whales. We cannot know the purpose of everything. Nature is a mystery to us. Therefore, we act foolishly and destroy trees, plants, and animals. Many ayurvedic herbs and plants look to us like useless weeds. Out of ignorance we destroy them. But a knowledgeable ayurvedic physician knows how useful and significant they are.

"Man is dependent onNature for his very existence. Nature is an indispensable part of life on earth. Without Nature no creature, not man or anything else, can live. Therefore, it is one of our foremost duties to lovingly care for all living things. You may feel that destroying a tree or a plant is a lesser wrong than killing a human being. This concept is wrong.Plants andtrees also have emotions and can feel fear. When somebody approaches a tree or plant with an ax or a hacking knife, the plant is afraid; it trembles with fear. You need to have a subtle ear to hear its cries, a subtle eye to see its helplessness, and you need a subtle mind to feel its fear. You do not see its suffering, but you can feel it if you have a compassionate heart. In order to see the suffering of a plant, your mind's eye must be open. Unfortunately, you do not see subtle things with your external eyes. Because of this, you destroy a helpless tree or plant.

"It has been scientifically proven that not only humans and animals, but plants and trees also have feelings and emotions. They can even express themselves to a certain extent; and if we have the right attitude, we can learn to understand. Ages ago, the saints and sages of India, having delved deep into the laboratory of their own consciousness, proclaimed that plants and trees also have feelings and that they could express their feelings if one had a loving and compassionate attitude towards them.

"Thestory ofShakuntala is a very good illustration of this point. Shakuntala was the adopted child of a sage named Kanwa. From a very young age, Shakuntala had a spontaneous love for Nature, for animals, plants, and trees. She loved them and cared for them like her own life. Every day Shakuntala watered the plants and bushes around the hermitage and spent much time in the garden expressing her love for them. She would even caress and kiss the plants. She expressed the same love for animals and birds, too. There was one jasmine plant in particular that she had a special attachment to and loved the most. She spent hours each day bathing its leaves and sniffing its lovely blossoms.

"Once a king came hunting in the forest. He happened to see Shakuntala and fell in love with her. The king and Shakuntala were married. It is said that on the day that Shakuntala left the hermitage, the plants and trees all bent low as if hanging their heads in sorrow. Shakuntala went up to each and every plant, tree, and animal and bade them good-bye with tear-filled eyes. The deer and the peacocks shed tears of great sorrow as Shakuntala took leave of them. And the jasmine plant, which she loved the most, even caught hold of Shakuntala's feet, wrapping its tendrils around them as if to prevent her from going."

Interrupting the profound flow of Her words, Mother looked at the mango tree. For some time Mother remained silent, Her gaze fixed on the tree. A few moments passed and She slipped into an indrawn mood. While Mother sat with Her eyes shut, tears ran down Her cheeks. Perhaps She was feeling compassion for the mango tree. Perhaps her tears were for something else which we can never know.

Don't be self centered

"Amma, we're sorry we were so careless," murmured one of the brahmacharis, his voice full of genuine regret. "We didn't mean to destroy the tree."

Opening Her eyes, Mother said, "What a pity it is that destruction has become the slogan of modern man. Nobody sincerely wishes for the good of another person. People have become veryself-centered and selfish. They want to destroy each other. They want to destroy everything. The thought of destruction comes when greed and selfishness overpower man.Love andcompassion are a uniting force. They alone can create a sense of oneness and cooperation. When man thinks only of himself and of his own desires, he becomes narrow. He becomes almost blind and sees nothing but himself and his utterly selfish little ego.

"Amma has heard a story about some young men who wanted to become the disciple of a certain spiritual master. The master took the would-be disciples to a well and asked each one to look inside and say what he saw. All but one of them said that they could see only their own reflection in the water. 'You don't see anything else?, the master asked once again. ' All replied 'No,' except for one young man who said, 'Yes, I, too, see my reflection in the water below, but along with it I see the reflection of the trees and plants that grow around the well.' The master accepted this young man as his disciple and told the others, 'You saw only your own image. That shows that you are self-centered. But this young man saw other things. He saw plants and trees as well. This shows that he is not self-centered. His vision is clearer than yours. It is him I will accept as my disciple.'

"Children, a self-centered person does not feel compassion or love. Such a person can become harmful to society. Such a person can easily and needlessly destroy. Wanton destruction is evil. Some countries have senselessly attacked other countries only out of the selfish desire to further their own interests. Selfishness, greed and self-centeredness are all evil. Evil can easily control human minds. Children, do not let evil overpower your mind. Willful destruction is sinful. Do not let sin overpower you. Absolutely lacking in feelings, a person with a destructive mind is obsessed with cruelty. Totally self-centered, he cannot see the oneness in everything, for he is unable to see or feel life in all things. Whatever he sees is 'other' than himself. Devoid of love and compassion, he cannot perceive the life in all things; he sees only inanimate matter. This attitude makes him destructive.

"A destructive person is filled with hatred and anger. Anger and hatred make humans blind, causing people to destroy each other. Everywhere in the world people are killing each other. That is what happens when the destructive force of anger and hatred takes over human minds. But the real nature of man is consciousness. Man is God, but he has forgotten this. What a pity! What a downfall! What degeneration!

"Once God was worried about three countries that were constantly at war. Each country wanted to destroy the other two countries and their people. Not only the leaders but even the people of the three countries hated one another. Eventually God called a meeting of the representatives of the three countries. God asked them, 'My dear children, why do you fight and quarrel like this? There is no peace anywhere, and people live in constant fear. Tell me, what do you want? Why do you fight, when I am here to fulfill all your desires? Come, if you have any problems, tell me. I will solve them, but no more destruction.' Then turning to the representative of the first country, God said, 'Tell me, what do you want?'

"The representative of the first country looked arrogantly at God and said, 'Look here, first of all we do not believe in Your existence. We have our own leaders that we believe in. If You want us to believe in You, You will have to give us proof of Your power.'

"'What proof do you want?' asked God. Pointing his finger at the ambassador of the second country, the representative of the first country said, 'Destroy him and his country. Destroy them totally. If You can do that, we will believe in You. We will build temples, churches and mosques for You, and we will encourage our people to worship You.'

"God was so taken aback to hear the desire of the first country, He was speechless. This silence of God persuaded the first representative to speak again. 'Okay,' he continued, 'it does not matter. Your silence means that You can't do it. That's okay. Since You can't do it, we will do it anyway. It might take us a little longer, but that's no problem.'

"Now God turned to the representative of the second country. The people of the second country were believers, so God thought he would respond in a more decent and agreeable manner. However, when God asked him what his country wanted, the ambassador said, 'My Lord, our desire is very small. We simply don't want to see any place for our friend, the first country, on the map. Just take their country out. Remove it, and leave only a blank space there. We don't want the name of our friend on the map. However, my Lord, if you do not do it with Your Grace and blessings, we will definitely do it with our armies in Your name.'

"This time God was really shocked. If even those who had faith in Him talked in this way, what would be the attitude of those who didn't? For some time He was struck dumb. Finally, with great hope, He turned to the representative of the third country, who looked very polite and gentlemanly. The representative of the third country smiled at God and greeted Him with joined palms. This gesture filled God's heart with optimism. He sighed and thought, 'At least he understands Me. Now I will be able to feel happy and content thinking that I can at least save one country from the path of destruction.' Returning the smile, God asked, 'Yes, my son, what is your wish?'

"The representative of the third country once again bowed down to God and coolly said, 'Divine Lord, we have no desire of our own. Be compassionate and fulfill the desires of both these countries; then our desire will also be fulfilled!'

"Such is the attitude of every country, every human being. Destruction, destruction, destruction. Children, stop destroying! This is not your path. Yours is the path of love and compassion.

Yours is the path of empathy, of feeling the pain and happiness of others as your very own."

Gayatri brought a drink for Mother, but She refused it, saying, "Amma does not feel like drinking or eating after seeing what Her children have done. Their thoughtless and indiscriminate act has created great pain in Her heart." Turning to the brahmacharis, she continued, "Due to your wrong judgment, you have destroyed a life. You should repent. You must not commit another mistake like this. But since you don't feel any concern for the life you have unnecessarily destroyed, Amma does not feel like eating or drinking today."

The thought that Mother was not going to eat or drink because of them made the brahmacharis feel remorseful and extremely sad. They never thought the course of events would take such a sharp turn. When Mother had begun to tell stories, the brahmacharis all thought the mango tree incident was over, that there would be no more fuss. But Mother's declaration upset them all over again.

Mother once again went up to the tree. This time She embraced it and kissed its trunk. As if addressing the very life of the tree or some deity which presided over it, She spoke, "My children acted indiscriminately. They are ignorant children. I consider it my own fault. How can it be otherwise? I have not taught them well enough for them to understand and feel that there is life in all of creation. I seek your forgiveness on my children's behalf. Forgive them for their ignorant act." Mother once again embraced the tree and kissed it before walking directly back to the Ashram.

Mother's strange but magnificent act provided everyone present with a great example of humility and love. The brahmacharis and the residents all felt very ashamed. They never would have imagined that someone would apologize to and seek forgiveness from a tree. Who but a person who beholds life everywhere could do such a thing? Who can set such an example of humility and compassion but one who is filled with love and compassion, a person who is constantly established in that supreme state? How could one who sincerely wants to follow the path of spirituality ever forget this event? Special lessons or experiences with Mother, the unusual things that She does, are never forgotten. The memory of such events and incidents are treasured forever in a sadhak's heart, in the innermost recesses of his very being.

Desperate with remorse, the brahmacharis followed Mother, saying, "Amma don't fast! We won't make this mistake again. Amma, please don't fast. We will not do such a thing again. Amma."

Mother seemed deaf to their pleas. She was about to climb the stairs to Her room when suddenly Nedumudi, the brahmachari whose idea it had been to move the tree, burst into tears. He cried and called to Mother, "Forgive me! I will never make a mistake like this again. From now on I will not do anything without seeking your advice. It was all my fault, Amma. You have taught me a good lesson. Please don't fast, Amma! I will fast on my own for as many days as you say. But please, Amma, please, you must not torture your body. I should suffer! I should be the one to suffer! Even when You shed tears, and sought the tree's forgiveness, I was unmoved. What an ego I have! What a sinner I am!" He started beating his head with his hands.

At the sight of the brahmachari's anguish, Mother's heart melted. She turned towards him and caught hold of both his hands. "Son... son... Amma's darling son. Don't worry. Amma will not fast. Do not beat yourself. You have repented enough. Now calm down. Amma will eat."

The above event is a very good illustration of the way Mother punishes Her children for their mistakes. In fact, one cannot call it punishment, for the word punishment is too negative to use in this context. Mother does not penalize Her children. Her way is simply to make them aware of their mistakes. Once the realization "I have committed this mistake, I should not have done it, I must repent" comes, then one is on the right track. In order to repair or make up for a mistake, one must first become aware of it. Without realizing that one has made a mistake or that one has a particular weakness that will become a stumbling block on one's path, how can one overcome or remove it?

Mother shows us our weaknesses and mistakes. She does not always wait for us to realize on our own the areas where we need work, but creates the circumstances necessary to make us realize our weaknesses on our own. And that She does by setting an example. One who witnesses and absorbs such an example cannot easily make the same mistake again. The examples and profound advice that Mother gives help a seeker to be more alert and careful; they inspire him to use his discrimination before performing any task or making any decision. Thus Mother's so-calledpunishments serve as precious experiences which guide Her children along the right path. Mother's lessons cannot really be called "punishments." They are actually blessings. Mother's scoldings or punishments are Her flowing to the sadhak in that form.

Mother sat down on the last step of the staircase. Covering his face with his hands, Nedumudi continued to weep. Compassion filled Mother's eyes as She affectionately rubbed his head. Gayatri was still holding the drink she had brought for Mother. Mother now took the drink from Gayatri and had a sip. Raising the crying brahmachari's face, Mother poured some of the water into his mouth. She then did the same with all the others and soon everyone was smiling. All were happy to have Mother's blessing and to know that She was not going to fast. Mother smiled at everyone again and said, "Children, everyone's mind is turbulent now, let us calm ourselves." Mother then began to sing

Paurnami ravil

O Mother,
You are the splendor of moonlight
Shining forth in the sky on a full moon night;
You are a spring evening,

Arriving in a beautiful, fragrant palanquin
Covered with flowers.

O Mother,
You are the exquisite sound
Awakening in the gentle strings of a tambura;
You are a lyrical poem
Within the bursting imagination of a poet.

You are the One in whom the seven primary colors
And seven notes have merged;
You are the fragrance of a flower,
The beauty of a rainbow,
And the coolness of a breeze.

The atmosphere once again grew calm and peaceful and everyone was left with the memory of yet one more wonderful experience worthy of contemplation.

A Mahatma cannot destroy

Saturday, 15 September 1984

The morningmeditation was going on. Mother was sitting among the coconut trees, surrounded by the Ashram residents. Mother kept a close watch on everyone to see if they were meditating with propersraddha. Even when, at nine-thirty, the time for meditation ended, no one stirred. No one spoke for a while. Moments passed, then one of the brahmacharis raised a question, "Amma, you said that one cannot destroy life if one has love and compassion. ButKrishna andRama killed many people.Jesus lashed the merchants who did business in the temple. These Masters are known as the embodiments of love and compassion, yet they did harm to life. Isn't this a contradiction?"

"First of all," Mother began, "you should remember that Rama and Krishna were not only Perfect Beings; they were kings too. Rama was a king and Krishna a maker of kings. As the rulers of their countries, it was their first and foremost duty to protect their countries and people from danger. Whenever and wherever there was a threat to righteousness, they had to fight to destroy the unrighteous and evil forces. But they fought only against cruel kings and evil forces.

"Rama and Krishna were embodiments of Universal Power. They were God's power in human form and thus had the power to create, sustain, and destroy. You say that they destroyed life. But don't you know that they also created and sustained life? Many such incidents are narrated in the great epics. We have neither the power to create nor to sustain, yet we go on destroying, always seeking excuses for our actions. Seeing that other people are doing the same as we are, we think we can justify even our worst actions. We feel that what we do is justifiable, if we can accuse a superior person of doing the same thing. We know we do wrong, but we have to find someone else to blame. It is ridiculous to blame God for our mistakes. God is the Creator, the Creator of the entire universe, while man is His creation. God is all-powerful, all-pervading, and all-knowing, whereas man is limited, confined as he is by his body, mind, and intellect. While God or the Guru acts out of complete and pure knowledge, man acts out of ignorance.

"Rama, Krishna, and Jesus were all-powerful, all-pervading, and all-knowing. When you say that Krishna killed, you are forgetting that He also gave life. Do you recall how He brought Arjuna's grandson back to life? The child was born dead, but Krishna gave the child life. It was the same Krishna who bestowed the ultimate fulfillment of human birth, emancipation, on the hunter whose arrow killed Krishna's body. It is said that the people who were killed by Him were all freed eternally from the cycle of birth and death.

"When you kill or destroy someone or something, you only lengthen the chain of your own karma. It is your destructive mind—your anger, hatred, selfishness or greed—that causes you to do such things. The anger or greed or selfishness in you persuades you to do evil, and that action adds more to your existing anger, greed and selfishness. It blows more air into the balloon of your ego, and you become more puffed up. Each time you act selfishly or angrily or greedily you are taking one more holiday, one more day of leave, from the state of perfection, from your eternal freedom.

"If you do not care how many births you take or how much you will have to suffer, that it is your choice. But you are harming other people. Not only by injuring or killing someone, but just by feeling angry, just by acting greedily or selfishly towards others, you are triggering the same negative feelings in them. Your negative feelings will invoke their negativity as well. They too will suffer, thereby adding to the storehouse of their karma, and will be born again with the additional vasanas that have been accumulated. Thus through your anger or selfishness, you have lengthened the chain of someone else's karma. You are responsible, since it happens due to your anger and greed. This is the kind of destruction you do.

"The same thing happens in the case of trees, plants, and other forms of life. When you destroy them, you are not doing it out of love and compassion. Mostly, it is out of anger, hatred, selfishness, or greed. Each time you destroy a plant or an animal, you are releasing one of these negative feelings in the form of vibrations. These negative vibrations cause that particular life form to suffer. What you give them will be returned. If you love them and feelcompassion towards them, the same sentiment will be returned. But if love and compassion are absent, can feelings exist other than negative ones? Some animals or snakes can strike back in revenge when man behaves cruelly. Some plants also have a certain degree of protection, but in general, plants and trees cannot defend themselves or strike back. They cannot express their anger, fear, or love, at least not in a way that most people can understand or perceive. Saints say that plants can express their feelings, but ordinary people cannot perceive them. Today, modern science has created instruments that can detect and register the feelings of plants, and in some cases even measure the intensity of such feelings. Thus, they have observed that through loveless actions and lack of compassion, plants also suffer. By harming them, you are lengthening theirkarma. Your selfishness blocks their evolution into a higher species of life and prevents them from attaining eternal freedom. Children, what do you think? Aren't you harming them?"

Mother paused as a devotee namedSarasamma came and prostrated before Her. Sarasamma began complaining about her son who she felt was very disobedient. As she spoke, the woman cried and placed her head on Mother's shoulder. "Daughter, don't worry," Mother said. He will be all right. It is just because of his age that he acts in this way. He is entering his teens, isn't he? Then this is how he should be now. This is the period when the immature ego is at its peak. At this time of life young people begin to feel that they can stand on their own two feet. They feel they do not need anyone's advice or guidance. They start feeling that their parents and society have been controlling them for all these years and now they want to be free. The boy just wants to be independent. He does not want to listen to or obey anyone. No advice can enter his mind. He becomes so arrogant that he closes his heart and is not open to anything. He thinks he already knows everything. He now feels that life until this point was filled with darkness, that he was locked in a prison by his parents and now he is free. Now he is like a newly-blossomed flower with its head held high. The flower doesn't know that it will soon wither away and its head will droop. Like this the arrogant teenager walks around with an air of pride, disobeying everybody and rejecting everything. But when he enters real life, his ego will be crushed. He will be forced to lower his head. Life will teach him lessons. After a while his ego will be mature, and he will have a better understanding of life. He will be humbled then; he will learn to obey.

"When a newly-recruited police officer reports for his initial duty on the streets, he will be terribly puffed-up. His arrogance may lead him to commit blunders such as catching the wrong person, or beating someone without good reason. He puts on a big show of his power. It goes to his head and makes him blind. This is quite natural. But he will soon learn his lesson from experience. If you meet the same policeman a few years later, he will be different; you may not even recognize him. His ego will have gained greater maturity, and thus, his whole personality and appearance will have changed. Life will beat you up until you learn your lessons.

"Daughter, the same is the case with your boy. Don't feel over-agitated and frightened about him. He is like a newly recruited policeman." Everybody laughed, even Sarasamma.

"He will be all right soon," Mother continued. Just wait. Have a little more patience. And be sure to send him here. Tell him that Amma would like to see him."

"He will definitely come when he hears that Amma has called him." Sarasamma looked happy; it was clear that she felt consoled.

When Sarasamma stopped talking, Mother suddenly left the normal plane of consciousness for another world. With arms out-stretched She began to sing

Chintakalkkantyam

O Glorious Light of Eternal Bliss
That dawns within when all thoughts subside,
I have happily surrendered everything
And am contemplating Your Golden Feet.

When You are there with me as my very own,
I have no need of other relatives;
I will quickly eliminate the ignorance of selfishness;
This mind will not be sad any more,
For it has shed the flower of desire.
Let the mind dissolve in brilliant luster
And enjoy eternal Peace.

Please come and dwell within me;
Help me live like the air,
In contact with everything
But bound to nothing.
O man, think!
Are you not living like an animal?
What is the real purpose of your life?

When the song was over and she had regained her normal consciousness, one of the brahmacharis spoke. "Amma, I don't think you finished answering the question aboutRama andKrishna destroying life.

"Yes, that is right," Mother continued, "You say that like others, Mahatmas destroy life. But they cannot destroy life. The Mahatmas are great saviors of mankind and of the entire creation. Even when they kill or destroy, what they are really doing is purifying and saving. Any destruction they do is only on the surface. They cannot kill or destroy because they have no egos. They are consciousness. Consciousness cannot kill or destroy. Only a person with an ego can kill and destroy.

"When Rama or Krishna killed someone, they did not feel any anger or hatred. As always, they were totally selfless and detached. Even then they were full of love and compassion. Though one may have seen a fierce form outside, hidden behind that was infinite love and compassion. A Mahatma is not attached to his body. The body may get angry but the Self does not. He is just a witness. Theanger and fierce external form that you see is a facade. Mahatmas are filled with divine energy and vibrations, and only that can be released. They do not even have to release this divine energy because that is simply what they are. Even while breathing his last, the Lord's victim feels this divine energy. He becomes peaceful and calm. He merges with the Lord or attains a superior birth, a noble birth endowed with noble qualities.

"If the victim were to feel anger or hatred towards the Lord, even that would not create another circle of karma for them because the Lord is consciousness. Their negative feelings are released without creating an impact on the other end; and so, no chain of negativity is formed. The feelings just merge in space, in consciousness. Thus, even when releasing the energy of anger and hatred, the victims' egos melt and disappear and their souls are purified and transformed. At that time, their vasanas are exhausted and they either transcend the cycle of karma or gain a higher birth. Once the vasanas are exhausted the soul is free from all worldly bondage.

"So, there is no comparison between the killing or destruction done by a Mahatma and that done by an ordinary mortal. Mahatmas bless their victims, either with a new and higher birth, or sometimes even with liberation. And so their so-called killing or destruction can only be considered as a blessing. The Mahatma is the real savior and human beings are the real destroyers. Even if a Mahatma cuts down a tree or a plant, even if he or she injures or harms someone, it is uplifting; the victim is actually being helped, he is being carried to a higher plane of consciousness. Because we are looking at it from the outside, we see only the harm that is done. Only when through spiritual practices we develop a subtle eye and a subtle mind can we see the great service that a Mahatma does through his so-called killing. What they kill is the ego only, freeing the individual self from the clutches of negativity. Because the transformation or purification that occurs in their presence and through their actions is so subtle, to see and understand a Mahatma's actions requires a subtle eye and a subtle mind. Blinded as we are by our egos, we cannot really behold what they do. The external eye is the eye of ego. The real eye is the inner eye, the eye of the mind of minds. That eye alone will help us to see through."

Mother got up and climbed the stairs to Her room. Gayatri followed while the brahmacharis stood below, their eyes fixed on Mother as She moved up the stairs. Even after She disappeared from sight, they remained motionless, basking in the lingering radiance of Her being.

Chapter 8

Mother remembers everyone

Thursday, 20 September, 1984

As if to demonstrate that, as Mother had said, Mahatmas are the saviors of life in all its forms, the transplanted mango tree sprouted new leaves. Everyone had thought that the tree was dead. It had shed all its leaves and its young trunk had gone limp. Then suddenly after receiving Mother's attention, the tree slowly began to show signs of life. And now, to everyone's great relief, it was again looking healthy and well. Only now did the residents realize the significance of Mother's embracing and kissing the tree. In doing so, She must have transmitted new life into it. Who can understand the meaning of a Mahatma's actions unless they themselves reveal it to us?

On this day a devotee who was not able to come to the Ashram very often arrived and said to Mother, "I am physically away from you most of the time. I rarely see you more than once a month. When I am not here, Amma, do you ever remember me?"

"Amma remembers everyone!" She laughingly replied. "How can Amma forget anyone, when the whole universe is within Her? You are all parts of Amma. How can the whole forget the part? The part exists in the whole. The part may think it is different from the whole, but the whole, which is the soul of everything, knows that the part is not different from it. That Supreme Soul is pure and transcendent love; it cannot see the part as different from Itself, so there can be no question of forgetting. Amma always remembers you, but your remembrance of Amma is equally important. When you remember that you are Amma's child, Amma's son or daughter, Amma's disciple or devotee, when you remember that She is always with you, that She sees all your actions and is your sole protector and guide, you are remembering the whole–you are recalling your real nature and true abode.

"Spiritual practices likemeditation andprayer are also remembrance of the Whole; they too are the remembrance of God in whom you exist. Spiritual practice reminds you, 'I am not just a part, but the part of the Whole–indeed, I am one with the whole.' All prayers and remembrance of God or Guru remind you of the great truth that you are not a separate entity, that you are not just a limited individual, but that you are His, that you are He.' When this loving remembrance arises within, you can never be away from Amma, nor can Amma ever be away from you.

"A person who is blinded by ego will forget others, because he is selfish. Having no concern or compassion for others, he lives in a small world of his own and sees everything as different from himself. He and everyone else are separate entities as far as he is concerned. He sees the many and thus cannot see life as a whole. But aMahatma's vision is entirely different. Having emptied his mind completely and filled it with love and compassion, he is egoless. He is wide awake and His all-pervading consciousness sees and hears everything. Everything happens within him. Within him, the entire universe exists. He is the universe. This is the meaning of the *Viswarupa Darshana* of Lord Krishna.[7] Nothing is

---

[7] The *Vishwarupa Darshana* took place during Lord Sri Krishna's discourse to Arjuna in the *Bhagavad Gita* which is part of the epic *Mahabharata*. The Lord revealed to Arjuna in a mystic vision that He was the entire universe; the sun

different from him. Realizing his oneness with the entire creation, he beholds everything as his own, as his own Self.

"Mahatmas live in love andcompassion. Forgetting their individual existence and sacrificing all bodily comforts, they not only love and constantly remember others, but they also selflessly serve the world. As they are dead to the ego, they cannot think of their own happiness or comfort. Therefore, son, questions such as yours have no significance. Your wife, children, parents and friends can forget you. Go away for some time and they will forget you. When a husband dies, the wife may cry, remembering the sweet times she spent with her husband. But she will soon learn to forget him and may even marry someone else. And when a wife dies, the husband will act in this same way.

Because people are limited, egoistic and selfish, this is bound to happen in all worldly relationships. Ordinary people, who are under the great pressure of their vasanas, are bound to forget. After the death of a wife or husband, any remembrance will probably be observed on an annual Memorial Day. Or the large, elaborately framed photograph on the mantle of the fireplace might invoke some memories once in a blue moon. With a sigh you might murmur, 'Ah, he (she) was a good person, but what can I do? I'm helpless. I must live, so I've found another partner. There was pressure from all sides.' Finished. Remembrance is over! Between each remembrance is a long interval of forgetfulness.

"But a Mahatma is beyond all such weakness. His heart is as big as the universe. He is infinite space which can contain everything and everybody. He is not sleeping. He is fully awake and therefore, he cannot forget.

"Son, Amma remembers you, not only you but everyone. How can Amma forget anyone when She is within them? Stop

---

was His eye, the moon was His mind and so on. Arjuna saw that every form was a form of God.

doubting and try to go beyond your limited vision. Don't ask, 'Do you ever remember me?' Don't think that you are physically away from Amma, or that you see Amma only once a month. These are only questions and doubts asked by your mind. Stop listening to your mind and you will feel Amma right there in your heart. Then you will know that Amma has never ever forgotten you, that you have always existed in Her and always will.

"Listen to this story: A lover came and knocked at the door of his beloved. 'Who's there?' asked the beloved from within. 'It is I,' said the lover. 'Go away. This home cannot hold both you and me.' Feeling terribly dejected, the rejected lover went away. For months on end he lived alone, pondering over and contemplating the words of his beloved. At last, one day he returned and knocked again at his beloved's door. 'Who knocks?' came a voice from within. 'It is you,' was the reply: And the door immediately opened.

"Love cannot contain two. It can contain only one. Love is *purnam* (fullness). In Love's constant and devoted remembrance, 'you' and 'I' dissolve and disappear. Love alone remains. The entire universe is contained in that pure, undivided Love. Love is endless; nothing can be excluded from it. Love is all-pervasive."

This statement shows Mother's real nature which is as big as the universe. "I see the entire universe as a small bubble within Me," says Mother. Infinity is Mother's nature. In the song, *Ananda Vidhi*, Mother describes the state of realization, "From that moment onwards, I could not see anything as different from my own Self. Merging in that bliss of eternal union with the Supreme Shakti, I renounced the world with all its objects." The state of supreme renunciation is the state of the highest detachment. In that state one goes beyond all form, one loses all individual consciousness and becomes one with Infinity.

"If you always remember Amma and you love Her, that is sufficient. It is enough if you can remember Her sincerely and intensely just once a day," Mother continued. "Son, where there is love there is no distance or separation. It is yourlove for Amma that keeps you close to Her. Whether or not you love Her, whether or not you're able to feel Her love, Amma loves you and She is with you. But you will feel Her closeness or presence only when you love Her. LordKrishna used to dance ecstatically on the banks of the river Yamuna with the Gopis of Vrindavan. One day Krishna suddenly disappeared and did not return for a long time. TheGopis were plunged into great sorrow. Some cried aloud, some fainted, and still others called out "Krishna, Krishna, Krishna!" as if they'd gone mad. At last, late in the night, the Lord returned. Forgetting themselves, the Gopis ran towards Him and pleaded, 'O Krishna, You who are so affectionate to Your devotees, why did You punish us like this? Why did You disappear, leaving us all alone? Isn't our love for You pure enough? O Krishna, You are our beloved Lord and God. Please do not forsake these Gopis who have no refuge other than Your Lotus Feet.'

"Krishna smiled and replied, 'Beloved ones, how can I be away from you, you who are so filled with love for Me? Even the air you breath is filled with My name and form. Even your heartbeats sing My praise. Dear gopis, where there is pure and innocentlove, there is no difference, there is no distance. Though the sun shines way up in the sky, the lotuses in the ponds on earth still bloom. Like this, the lotuses of your hearts have blossomed fully in the sunshine of your love for Me. We are forever one.' Likewise, children, how can there be any feeling of difference or distance when you constantly remember Amma with love and devotion? Mother is within you and you are within Mother."

Hearing Mother's soothing words, the devotee felt very happy and gazed at Mother with a smile of joy on his face. He then expressed a wish to sing to Mother. The song he sang was

Orunalil varumo

O Mother of unearthly Bliss,
Will You come, one day, soon,
To the shrine of my heart
With Your eternally shining lamp?
It is for this reason alone
That this supplicant is wandering about.

O Devi, won't You bless me
With a melting heart?
I have searched for the Divine Mother everywhere.

O Mother, bestow Your Grace upon me
Caress me with Your soft hands
O Mother, give me shelter.

I am falling with exhaustion.
I know the truth that You dwell within me,
But when will the day of Realization come?

Selflessness and intellect

Saturday, 22 September, 1984

Late in the afternoon Mother was sitting in the coconut grove with some of the brahmacharis, Gayatri, Kunjumol and a few devotees. One of the brahmacharis asked a question, "Amma, does a person who is doingselfless action need to do anysadhana?"

"Children," Mother began, "completeselflessness is possible only after the attainment of Self-Realization. All actions that we call 'selfless' before the attainment of that state are merely attempts to reach the ultimate state of selflessness. Selfless action is possible only when the ego is completely uprooted. Until then, all actions will be tainted with selfishness. You may think that what you have done is 'selfless,' but if you look a little deeper you will find that there is always a hidden motivation of self-interest.

"Children, selflessness is the goal to be attained.Action coupled with meditation, japa, chanting, and otherspiritual practices are the means to attain the state of selflessness. There should always be a balance between meditation and action. Action alone cannot take you to the goal. Action performed with an attitude of self-surrender and love is the right path. Action should be well-rooted in the essential principles of spirituality, otherwise it will not take you to the goal. Only action performed with the right attitude can take you to the state of selflessness.

"We see people working. Work alone cannot make people selfless. They work to earn their livelihood. They work in order to gain honor, status and position, thus their work will only strengthen their egos. Such work becomes food for the ego. They have desires to fulfill, for they still have a heap of vasanas within. Their outlook on action is totally different from a sadhak's. It has nothing to do with spirituality and its essential principles. Such desire-prompted action cannot lead you to selflessness. It cannot help you dive deep into meditation because selfish action creates more mental waves, morevasanas, and more desires. Only action performed with an attitude of selflessness can help you to go deeper into meditation. And realmeditation will happen only when you have become truly selfless, because it is selflessness that removes thoughts and takes you deep into the silence.

"Action performed with a spirit of selflessness is far superior to action performed with selfish motives. A person who is inspired by the ideal of selflessness is less attached to the action and more dedicated to the ideal of selflessness. This attitude of selflessness has a beauty of its own. As you feel the bliss and joy of selfless action more and more, you enter deeper and deeper into a state of selflessness and meditation. So in the beginning, just feel inspired by that very ideal. Love the ideal; be inspired by it. In the beginning it is a conscious and deliberate attempt. As you feel more and more inspired by the ideal of selflessness, you start working from your heart. By the very performance of the work, a joy will spring forth from deep within you. Eventually it will become spontaneous. Along with doing selfless action, one should also find enough time to contemplate, meditate and pray. As you try to perform selfless actions, friction and conflicts are bound to occur. It is inevitable for these things to come up, especially when you work in a group. Friction and conflict will sometimes cause your mind to be agitated. This, in turn, might cause your enthusiasm and vigor to diminish, and you may feel less inspired by the ideal of selflessness. Anger, hatred and thoughts of vengeance are bound to arise. In order to remove all such negative feelings and in order to keep yourself always in the right spirit, you must meditate, pray and contemplate. You should not let any thoughts block your spiritual growth. You should not have any ill feelings towards anyone.

"Children, because in our present state of mind, our so-called 'selfless' actions are not always completely selfless, we must try to keep a perfect balance between action and meditation. Introspection, contemplation, prayer, and chanting are necessary in the beginning stages of spiritual life. As we grow in our attitude of selflessness, our meditation will become deeper and deeper.

Another brahmachari asked, "Amma, can proper intellectual understanding take one to the state of Self-Realization? Or is it just a question of undivided faith and pure, innocent love?"

Mother smiled, "Children, a person endowed with proper intellectual understanding can no more be called 'an intellectual,' because proper intellectual understanding means proper discrimination, or *viveka*. Viveka helps you see clearly and to penetrate into the things and events which surround you.

"A person who only uses his intellect, who takes pride in his intellect, is a person with an obsessed personality. Whether he is right or wrong, he strongly believes that his point of view is correct, that what he sees is right. Such a person cannot listen to or hear what others feel about something. Even when someone else is speaking, he will continue to speak within. He is filled with ideas and information; and he is always waiting for the other person to stop speaking so that he can start. He does not listen; he absorbs nothing. Such people cannot surrender. Being restless and confused, they cannot pray or meditate. One will find it very difficult to be with them, for they can easily anger people and make enemies. It is difficult for them to believe in God or a Guru because they cannot accept someone else as their superior. Such a person will say, 'I am my own boss.' He is stuck in his intellect and cannot see or go beyond it. To go beyond one needs faith. Most intellectual people are coiled up in a shell of their own creation. They cannot come out of it, for they feel secure there. Outside the shell, they feel very insecure. They have their own concepts and theories, and are keen on expounding them. A person who relies solely on his intellect cannot surrender in complete acceptance unless a serious danger, a threat to his life or a near-death experience, confronts him. Only in the face of a serious threat is there a chance that he might call out for God.

Unless one surrenders, how can one open up? How can one see the reality behind things?"

Mother continued, "A few months ago Amma visited a house in which the wife was a good devotee who still comes to the Ashram today. When she first came to see Amma, this woman was undergoing many difficulties because of her husband, a professor of philosophy. As a non-believer and a skeptic, he would not let his wife and children pray or meditate. He had issued strict orders not to have any pictures of gods and goddesses in the house. He had also forbidden his family to read religious texts. His wife and their two daughters suffered greatly under his restrictions.

"It was while the husband was away on a lecture tour that this woman and her two children first came to see Amma. The woman and her children wept as they told Amma all about the difficulties they had been having at home. During the period of his absence they made several more visits to the Ashram and grew more and more devoted to Amma.

"When the husband returned, he learned that his wife and children had visited the Ashram. He was furious, and from that point on he became even more controlling about where they went and what they did. The family suffered terribly, and found it difficult to openly express their love and devotion to Amma. They lived under his tyranny until suddenly he was diagnosed with lung cancer. He soon became completely bedridden, and was not able to eat or sleep because of intense pain.

"Unable to bear the sight of her husband's agony, the wife came to the Ashram and told Amma that her husband had lung cancer and was suffering from unbearable pain. With great hesitation, she told Amma that her husband had expressed a desire to see Her. She hesitated because she thought Amma would never think of coming to see anyone who was so critical about religion and God. So, she was very surprised when Amma readily agreed to visit her husband. Amma never had any bad feelings about this son. She sympathized with his nature and had only love and compassion for him. Even when his wife had only complaints about him, Amma never advised her to go against her husband's wishes. Amma would tell her, 'Daughter, have patience and love. Only your love and patience can change him.' Amma believes the wife understood and followed this advice.

"Amma was only too happy to go and see this suffering son. When the man saw Her, he was completely humbled and full of remorse. Keeping Amma's hands on his chest and sometimes on his face, he cried like a small child. He must have apologized to Amma a hundred times for his faults. After Amma's visit he became very peaceful and relaxed, and always kept a picture of Amma on his chest. His wife said to Amma that after Amma's visit he never suffered again from pain. He could eat and sleep comfortably, and was very much at peace. Every day he used to apply Amma's sacred ash all over his body. His eyes full of tears, he would often pray to Amma seeking Her forgiveness. He had been extremely afraid of death before he met Amma. But after seeing Her, he was relaxed and calm; the prospect of his own death no longer filled him with fear. He is still alive, and is today a transformed and devoted person."

Everybody sat in silence after Mother concluded this story. They felt fortunate to be in the compassionate presence of a Mahatma. Mahatmas are compassionate even to those who oppose them and are disagreeable towards them. Their compassion is beyond all differences. That is whyKrishna bestowed the final state of emancipation even on the hunter whose arrows put an end to His body. That is whyRama could smilingly renounce his royal position and kingly pleasures without a shred of anger or hatred towardsKaikeyi, who issued the order that Rama should go and live in the forest for fourteen years. That is why Jesus could pray for those who crucified Him. It is for this same reason that Mother visited the professor who always abused Her.

Love is Mother's nature. She cannot be otherwise. Just as egotism is our present nature, egolessness is the nature of a Mahatma. A person's ego cannot affect a Mahatma, as there is nothing for it to hold on to. Egolessness is nothingness filled with love and compassion; it is nothingness filled with the presence of divinity. For this reason, Mother cannot return our anger, hatred or abuse. Mother can only bestow boundless love and compassion. Our anger, hatred and abuse dissolve and disappear in the ocean of Her of compassion. When we attack a Mahatma with the weapons of our anger and hatred, he or she fights back with the weapons of love and compassion. Eventually we will be disarmed, and the Mahatma will be victorious over us.

Mother continued, "In the professor's case, he feared that death was going to take his life. He thought he was going to die. He clearly understood that his intellect was useless. From that realization, real intelligence and discrimination arose. At one time he had considered his intellect as something great and invincible. However, this invincible intellect turned out to be utterly useless as the realization of death dawned in him. At this point he felt that he had been defeated. A defeated man has no claims to make. He is at the mercy of his conqueror; he can do nothing but surrender. Before he found out that he was ill, he was full of ego, drunk with himself, intoxicated by his power and position. He must have thought that he was great. 'Why should I bow down to anyone? How can I, a great professor of philosophy, accept the existence of God!' 'I' and 'mine' were his greatest friends. After realizing the inevitability of death, he was thrown down and completely humbled. There he lay, utterly defeated, saying, 'You, You alone can save me from this helpless state.'

"Once you realize that you are utterly helpless, you sincerely wish that someone will save you from this state. This wish to escape death is extremely intense. This is the greatest crisis of your life, and the wish to avoiddeath is the strongest desire you have ever had.

"In some people, intellect gives way to intelligence or discrimination at this point. The professor realized his helplessness and deeply regretted how he had been. He sincerely wished to see Amma, and that is why Amma had to go to him.

"When you become aware of your helplessness, your heart will be very open and receptive. You become very thirsty; your thirst is unquenchable. All your sense organs, all the pores of your body, are fully open to receive peace and love. The experience is akin to being trapped in a forest fire. Imagine such an experience. Think how you would act. You would want to get out of the fire. You would not have many thoughts. You do not pause to recollect sweet memories such as the day you met your wife, and at that fatal moment the future also disappears. You cannot stop to think of the arrangements that are to be made for your daughter's marriage or your son's birthday the following month. You live solely in the present because your life is at stake. You cannot think of anything but the safety of your own life. And at that moment, for the first time ever, you are wide awake. Up until then you were asleep. You were sleeping either in past memories or in future promises and dreams. You were never awake to the present. But now, when there is the urgency of a great threat, you must be awake for at least some time, otherwise you will die.

"When two warriors fight, both are wide awake. Having developed a subtle eye, they are aware of every movement. This awareness comes suddenly. A bat of his opponent's eye and the warrior will lunge forward with his sword. They are fully awake and alert. In the moment of danger they die to their past and future and live entirely in the present. When faced with a great threat, we become like these warriors. We too surrender to the present in the face of death.

"Children, surrender comes through the realization of your own helplessness. The realization that all that you claim as yours–your intellect, beauty and charm, your health and wealth–are nothing before the great and imminent threat of death. Death will snatch everything away. This realization wakes you up. You become alert. You realize that you are laying claim on things which are not really yours. Therefore, surrender. You can enjoy life's many pleasures, but you should do so with the awareness that it may all be taken away at any time. If you live life with this awareness, surrender will follow.

"There was once a great emperor who set out to conquer the world. He waged one war after another, amassing a vast amount of wealth by looting every country and then making the people pay high taxes. He was a powerful ruler, but selfish and cruel. Greedy for acquisitions, he was considered the richest man on earth. But death calls even the powerful and wealthy. When this great emperor was dying, he reflected, 'To gain this empire I have committed so many evil deeds, all for the sake of power and wealth. Now death is approaching and I can I take nothing with me. I, the great warrior who set out to conquer the whole world, can take nothing with me when I die. When death calls, I have to leave everything–all the riches, the splendor of the court, the glory of the battlefield. I must go alone; I cannot take even a single coin.' He told his courtiers and attendants, 'When you prepare my body for burial, be sure that my two hands are stretched out and that my palms are open and fully exposed. Like this my subjects will see that I, a great emperor–the richest and most powerful man in the world–went completely empty-handed on my final journey.' This is a great truth. Whoever you are, whatever your position may be, in a moment's time death will grab everything, even your body. Therefore, surrender."

An extraordinary silence followed and lasted for sometime. Gradually, the mood drifted into a poignant song led by Br. Sreekumar

Kannadachalum

Whether my eyes are open or closed,
I constantly see my Mother;
Mother embraces one and all
Her every glance pours forth compassion
And by the flood of Her Love
Each heart is melted.

My Mother is an ocean of joy;
To Mother, both a robber and a tyrant
Are Her own darling children;
Whether She is despised or adored,
Love constantly streams from Mother.

Mother's life,
Befitting a descendant of the great sage Vyasa,
Illustrates that the Power of the universe
Can manifest
In a place as simple as a humble hut.

The tongue may enjoy the taste of sweetness,
But the senses are not perfect;
The Love of God is the perfect sweetness,
And that sweetness can be enjoyed through Mother.

Mother sat with Her eyes closed during the song. When it ended, everyone was silent for some time, waiting for some indication from Mother as to what would take place next. Mother opened Her eyes and flashed an endearing smile to all. When Mother smiles, it is so engaging, so all-encompassing that every single person present feels that She has looked deep into his or her very own heart. A child may feel that the sun is shining on him alone, following him wherever he goes, for every time he looks up, the sun is there, shining down on him. Mother's smile is like the sun that shines on all. And each person, like a child, feels that She is smiling at him or her alone.

The same brahmachari who had raised the doubt about intellect spoke again, "Amma, what is the conclusion? Is proper intellectual understanding helpful or not?"

Mother answered, "Proper understanding will help you realize that unless you drop the intellect you cannot reach the state of eternal freedom. Proper understanding will dawn only when you feel the burden of your ego, only when you feel the heaviness of the intellect. Only when you feel weighed down by the ego can you begin to unburden it. The ego makes you feel that you are great. Only when you are thrown into a helpless situation will you come to know that you are nothing. Death is the most helpless state of all. All big egotists and stubborn intellectuals have realized their helplessness while dying. Only a real blow to the ego or a serious threat can bestow this understanding. But once this understanding dawns, the intellectual obsession is removed and you are no longer a prisoner of the intellect and its reasoning. Viveka arises. Viveka gives you more clarity of vision. This clarity, in turn, helps you to realize the impermanent and transitory nature of the world. All the wealth and possessions you have accumulated are with you now and at your disposal. But within a flash they can all become someone else's. Later they will go to another person, and then to another one and then to yet another. Therefore, do not be full of ego, thinking that you are the owner of all this wealth. Life is a mystery. You cannot understand it unless yousurrender, for your intellect cannot grasp its expansive and infinite nature, its real meaning and fullness. Bow down low and behumble; then you will know life's meaning.

"Once the transitory nature of the world is understood, once this helplessness of the ego is realized,faith arises. Because you know then that you are nobody and a nothing in life, you realize that you want help from a supremely powerful being. This clinging to the Supreme Power leads you to faith and surrender. Properdiscrimination, which springs from proper understanding, will help you to develop faith and love. Through faith, self-surrender happens, and through self-surrender one can definitely attain the state of Self-Realization.

"Only the knowledge or realization that you know nothing can really help you to grow internally. Only a person with this knowledge is truly wise. Greatness lies inhumility, not in claiming to be great.

"Once the oracle of a city declared that a certain Mahatma was the wisest man in that city. When this news was reported to the Mahatma, he laughed and said, 'It must be a mistake. I do not know anything. In fact, the only thing I know is that I do not know anything, that I am ignorant.' The puzzled messenger returned to the oracle and told him what the Mahatma had said. 'That is why he is considered the wisest man in this city,' the oracle explained. 'Those who claim to be wise and knowledgeable are fools.'"

Without any warning, Mother's mood suddenly changed into that of a playful and innocent child. She stood up and picked an orange from a big bag of fruit that had been offered by one of the devotees. Putting the orange on Her head, and humming a

187

tune, Mother started to dance just like a little child. Next Mother put the orange on Her forehead and held it there as She continued to dance. Soon Mother's humming turned into a song, and everyone joined in

Chilanka Ketti

O my lotus-eyed One,
Tie on Your anklets and come running!
Come dancing!

We have come in search of Your tender Feet,
And we are singing Your divine Name.

O Devaki's Son, Radha's own Life,
O Kesava, Hare, Madhava,
O Slayer of Pootana,
Destroyer of sins,
Child of Gokula, come running!
O Cowherd Boy, come dancing!

O Slayer of Kamsa,
Who danced on the serpent Kaliya,
O Kesava, Hare, Madhava,
Who is affectionate to those taking refuge in You;
Protector of those in danger,
O Embodiment of OM,
Come running!
O Melody of Bliss,
Come dancing!

To the delight of everyone, Mother's enchanting dance went on for some time. Her innocent smile and sparkling eyes made Her look like a divine child, the embodiment of purity. To watch Her made the others long to become innocent like children; they also wanted to dance and play. Mother's innocence was so powerful and captivating that everyone was overwhelmed with love.

Eventually Mother stopped dancing. Still in the mood of a child, She took a handful of sand and made it into a ball. Soon She was walking around with the ball of wet sand balanced on Her forehead. Her head bent a little backwards, Mother tried not to let the ball of sand drop. This play went on for a while until finally the ball fell to the ground. Like a helpless child, Mother exclaimed, "Oh no, it broke!" and a disappointed expression crossed Her face.

The mishap with the ball of sand and Mother's funny, child-like look triggered a little laughter among the brahmacharis. Seeing that they were laughing, Mother's face changed. Now She looked a little angry. But even the anger of a child has a certain beauty. The next moment, with a lightning-quick movement of Her hands, Mother took some sand from the ground and threw it at the brahmacharis, and then She walked away.

Since She seems like an ordinary village girl, one may wonder at first how Mother could so suddenly and so completely transform Herself into a child. But if one looks a little deeper it is not hard to see the truth. How can various moods and roles be unnatural for one who is One with Infinity. Changing masks is a wonderful play for a great being like Mother. But it is a divine game, and can be played only by one who can discard or change the mask after it has served its purpose. There is never any sort of attachment to the mask.

There is an infinite number of masks that Mother may wear. Sometimes She wears the mask of a Great Master who talks about the profound truths of life. At other times She is the most loving and compassionate Mother of all. And at still other times, She is a great disciplinarian. Sometimes one can see Her playing the role of a great administrator who oversees even the most minute detail of the spiritual institution run by Her. And there are also occasions, like the one just described, when one can see Mother in the mood of an innocent child. But still, the truth remains that Mother is far beyond all this. And all these moods and leelas are possible only because She is the Beyond.

Chapter 9

A transcendent mood

Sunday, 30 June, 1984

Preparations for the celebration of Mother's thirty-second birthday were underway. Constant activity was going on everywhere in the Ashram. Devotees and the residents worked hand in hand cleaning the premises, filling in certain areas with sand, moving construction materials out of the way, and giving the buildings and the temple a fresh coat of paint.

Brahmachari Balu had prepared a special presentation to be given during the celebration. He wanted to narrate the life of a Mahatma with appropriate songs interwoven with the story. This kind of storytelling, famous in the temples of Kerala, is known as *Harikatha*. The word Harikatha means the story of the Lord. Balu's original plan had been to narrate Mother's life in this way, but Mother disagreed. "No, not when Amma is alive," She said. So the life of another Mahatma was chosen. But before performing it in front of an audience, Balu wished to have Mother approve and bless the project.

The opportunity soon arose. Mother, Balu, Rao, Sreekumar, Venu and Pai, were all sitting in Mother's room above the meditation hall. Mother was seated on Her cot, and the others were gathered around Her on the floor. Mother said She wanted to listen to the story. Sreekumar was soon ready with the harmonium and Venu quickly set up his *tablas*. Balu began, and Mother listened keenly to the story and the songs. At times She suggested a few changes here and there. Sometimes Mother felt that the dialogue was not very effective, and asked Balu to change a sentence or a few words. In other places Mother instructed Balu to replace one song with another one. And sometimes Mother even sang along.

At one point Balu was describing the Mahatma's intense longing to realize God. He was depicting the excruciating pain of separation from his beloved deity through the following song

Kera vrikshannale

O trees and creepers,
Have you seen my Mother?
O glittering stars,
Where has my Mother gone?

O birds of the night singing in the trees,
Did my Mother pass this way?
O Lady Night,
Where can I find my Mother?

I am wandering along every shore,
crying and seeking my Mother.
O my Beloved Mother,
I will ask every particle of sand
To tell me where You are.

Hearing these verses and their description of the intense yearning and agony of separation, Mother entered into a deep state of samadhi. At first She silently shed tears of bliss and then, suddenly, Mother burst into blissful laughter. After this had gone on for some time, in Her ecstasy, Mother began to roll very fast on the ground

like a spinning wheel. As She rolled around, Mother continued
to laugh. For some time, the brahmacharis watched in wonder
and awe. But when after a few minutes Mother showed no sign
of coming out of Her ecstatic mood, they began to worry. It was
not the first time that they had seen Mother like this, and in the
past, She Herself had instructed them to sing bhajans in order to
coax Her back to the normal plane of consciousness should She
remain in samadhi for more than a short while. And so, gathering in a corner of Mother's small room, the five brahmacharis
began quietly to sing

Nirvanashatkam (Manobuddhya)

I am not the mind, intellect, ego or memory;
I am not the taste of the tongue,
Or the sense of hearing, smell and sight;
I am not earth, fire, water, air or ether;
I am Pure Bliss Consciousness
I am Shiva, I am Shiva.

I am not right or wrong actions,
Nor am I pleasure or pain;
I am not the mantra or any sacred places,
The Vedas or the sacrifice;
I am not the act of eating, the eater or the food;
I am Pure Bliss Consciousness
I am Shiva, I am Shiva.

I have no birth or death,
Nor have I any fear;
I don't hold any caste distinction;
I have no father or mother,
Associates or friends;
I have no Guru

And I have no disciple;
I am Pure Bliss Consciousness
I am Shiva, I am Shiva.

I have no form,
Or movements of the mind;
I am the All-Pervasive;
I exist everywhere;
Yet I am beyond the senses;
I am not salvation,
Or anything that may be known;
I am Pure Bliss Consciousness
I am Shiva, I am Shiva.

In HerGod-intoxicated state, Mother continued to roll and laugh for ten or fifteen minutes. Finally She got up from the floor and began moving around the room as if drunk. Mother stumbled about with faltering steps, laughing blissfully all the while. Her fingers were held in identical divine mudras, and Her face glowed, emitting a penetrating radiance. Several times Mother's head or body came close to hitting the walls or banging against the floor, but the brahmacharis were very watchful and protected Her from any possible harm. For some time, Mother remained in one spot and gently swayed from side to side, reveling in Her own world, a world to which no one else had access. Eventually Mother lay down on the floor and remained still. The brahmacharis continued to sing until Mother had finally descended from Her exalted state.

Satya and dharma – Truth and righteousness

In the evening, Mother was sitting in front of Nealu's hut talking to a few devotees who had just arrived. One of them asked, "Amma, is it possible in this modern age to follow the examples set by great devotees and saints in the great epics of old? The incidents in those stories must have occurred thousands of years ago when *satya* (truth) and *dharma* and love for God were commonly observed. As people no longer place so much importance on truth and righteousness, are those examples applicable in today's world?

Mother replied, "Son, a doubting mind is a great hindrance to the observance of spiritual truths. We never learn to believe. We only learn to doubt. This is the greatest curse that humanity is confronting today. It is true that long ago satya and dharma were more predominant than they are now, and that prevalence made the atmosphere more conducive for devotion and spiritual practices. But satya and dharma are imperishable; they are indestructible and therefore they still exist. The difference is that in ages past people practiced those ideals, but now we do not. Yet, today it is still the observance of satya and dharma by at least a few souls that helps sustain the entire world.

"Son, you ask if this is applicable in modern society. There are still many people who observe the principles of satya and dharma. Even though they are a minority, you cannot deny the fact that they exist.

"Look at these children here in the Ashram. They are all very young and well-educated. Most of them are from well-to-do families. They had the courage and strength to renounce their old way of living and to embrace an entirely different lifestyle. They were leading normal lives in the world like all modern youths, but once they realized that spirituality is the highest truth, they fearlessly renounced their home. Their intense love for Amma and their longing to realize God enabled them to do this. Their love for the path of spirituality gave them courage and made them fearless. Their families, neighbors, and friends, and sometimes their entire village, criticized and abused them. Seeing their unusual behavior, people believed that they were crazy. People insulted and taunted them in public, but they could easily dismiss this ill-treatment and were never affected by insults or mean words. Because of their love and devotion they became so fearless that they could calmly stand before their parents and explain that they were going to embrace the path of spirituality, no matter what happened.

"Their families tried to tempt them back to worldly life, to the life of enjoyment and indulgence, which most people consider normal. But an indulgent person has no mental balance; he is actually abnormal, while a spiritual seeker, on the other hand, is well-balanced and therefore 'normal'. Thinking that their children had been hypnotized or that they were under an evil spell cast by this crazy girl, some of their families performed rituals to eliminate what they thought to be an evil power. They gave their children food laced with an antidote which these boys accepted and ate without fear. Some families even took them to psychiatrists to have them treated for mental illness. These boys willingly surrendered to everything with the strong faith that nothing bad would happen to them and that Amma would protect them from any harm. That faith saved them. They were fearless, not even afraid of death. They were mad with love for Amma and God and wanted to practice the principles of spirituality in their lives.

"One night, a group of hostile young men surroundedBalu when he walked out of the Ashram after the Krishna Bhava. It was dark, and the young men, who had been hiding somewhere, suddenly surrounded him. These village rowdies were adamantly opposed to Amma and the children who were devoted to Her. First they told Balu that he should stop singing bhajans in the Ashram. Then they said that he should stop coming to the Ashram at all. Some of them even wanted to beat him up. They egged each other on saying, 'Why do we waste time speaking to this rascal? You think he deserves special treatment? Let's beat him up!' They kept on abusing him, using harsh and crude words. But Balu remained silent; he felt no fear. He could have run away or shouted for help since this happened just outside the Ashram and devotees would surely have come to his aid. But he stood his ground and remained silent and calm.

"All their threats and efforts to provoke and scare him failed. In the end, one of the ruffians said that they would let him go, but that they would kill Balu and throw his body in the backwaters if they ever saw him in the village again. Balu was fearless and unmoved even by such a threat. He coolly and smilingly replied by telling them that he was not afraid. 'Mother has taught me that the Atman is imperishable,' he said. 'I have faith in Her. I have surrendered to Her. Nobody can stop me from coming here or from singing to Mother. If you want to beat me up or kill me, do it now. I will not raise even my little finger against you.' Having spoken, Balu closed his eyes and folded his arms across his chest. He expected that all of them together would jump on him like a pack of wild dogs. But nothing happened. In a few moments he opened his eyes to find that all the rascals had left. Where did Balu get his courage? How could he be so fearless and calm? It was because of his love and devotion. Wasn't he following the path of the great devotees and saints of old?

"Rao also underwent great difficulties. His family was dead set against his spiritual life and created many problems for him. They even took him to a mental hospital where he underwent ten days of shock treatment. Think of the great danger in giving shock treatment to a person who is not suffering from any sort of mental illness! It could have done serious damage to his brain. But Rao was fearless and let them do what they wanted, for he had strong faith that Amma would protect him. As it turned out, the treatment didn't do him any harm.

"Even today, many such incidents are taking place in peoples' lives. But you still doubt whether the observance of spiritual principles is possible in the modern age. Why shouldn't it be possible? Stop doubting and learn to believe, then you will see the possibility.

"Children, practice of spirituality is possible only through the knowledge that the Atman, the Self, cannot be harmed or killed. Only knowledge of the Self will lead one to the state of completefearlessness. The body must die because whatever is born must die. But the Atman was never born. It was always there; it is and always will be. There is nothing but the Atman, the Self, therefore it cannot be destroyed. This knowledge can completely free one from the grip of death and all the fear that goes along with it. A Mahatma is consciousness embodied. Having faith in a Mahatma, then, is equal to having faith in the infinite power of the Self.

"These boys were not Self-Realized souls, but their faith and love made them fearless. Only a fearless person, full of trust in God, can renounce everything, as they have done. All our attachments arise from fear. When you begin to penetrate through appearances, you will see that human beings live in constant fear. Fear prompts us to cling. Fear for our security bothers us constantly; if we have no money, fear grips us; if our wife leaves us, we feel fear; if we do not get a job, fear creeps in. Similarly, if we lose something–money, our home or our job–we experience fear. We feel safe and secure when we are attached to something, or if we have something in our hands. Attachment helps us temporarily to forget our fear; but deep down the fear remains.

"The people and objects that we are attached to must leave us one day. They cannot be with us forever. In due course they will disappear from our life. Our wife and children, our home and car, and everything that we are attached to will change or disappear.

And when each thing or person disappears we are again overcome by agony and fear. This will continue until we surrender to God and develop faith in the eternal nature of our real Self.

"Children, devotion to God and faith in the Atman are possible even today. All the calamities and problems that exist in the world come only from lack of faith and devotion, from a lack of love. Once we lose faith in a Supreme Controller, or God, there cannot be any harmony or peace in society. People will act and live as they like. Morality and ethics will disappear from the face of theearth. People will be tempted to live like animals. Absence of faith, love, patience and forgiveness make life hellish. 'More comfort... more comfort...' will be the aimof life. Selfishness and greed will overpower many, destroying their humanity.

"Children, the present world is almost like this already. There is an urgent need for people to observe and practice spiritual principles. That is the only way to save the world and the human race from destruction. Doubt will destroy all of our good tendencies. Put aside your doubts and call out for help to the Supreme Lord. Pray, meditate, and perform other spiritual practices. Everyone has a responsibility to save humanity. You, too, have a part to play. By doing your duty with the utmost sincerity and love, you are helping your own Self. You are saving your own life, which in turn will help society as well."

Everyone listened keenly to Mother's soul-stirring satsang. When Mother stopped speaking, Her audience sat in rapt silence, and it seemed that all of Nature was standing still. The silence between Mother's talks always created an inspiring atmosphere. Sometimes Mother withdrew from Her surroundings and sat deeply absorbed in Her own Self. This intensified the power of these deeply quiet moments, enhancing the presence of Divinity that already filled the air. As if to heighten the meditative mood, Mother asked the brahmacharis to sing

Kodanukodi

O eternal Truth,
For millions of years
Mankind has been searching for You.

The ancient sages renounced everything,
And for the purpose of making the Self flow,
Through meditation,
Into Your Divine Stream,
They performed endless years of austerities.

Your infinitesimal Flame,
Inaccessible to all,
Shines like the blaze of the sun;
It stands perfectly still, without a flutter
In the fierce wind of a cyclone.

The flowers and creepers,
The shrine rooms and temples,
With their newly installed sacred pillars,
Have been waiting for You for eons
And still You remain unreachable.

Fear of God

Soon after the song ended, another devotee asked, "Amma, when you explained that fearlessness is the sign of a true devotee, were you talking only about one who has dedicated his whole life to the search for God? What about an ordinary devotee? Do you think that a certain amount of fear, like the fear of God, is necessary for some devotees?"

"Children," Mother began, "fear is completely absent only when love is present in all its fullness. This kind of love is found only in a devotee who has surrendered completely to God. Such a devotee lives in love; he has drowned in the ocean of love. Fully consumed by Divine Love, his individual existence is lost, for he has merged with the totality of love. He becomes love. He becomes an offering to his Lord. Like a drop of water which falls into the sea and merges with its vast expanse, the devotee dives into the ocean of bliss as he offers himself to existence. In that state, all fear, all worries, all attachments and sorrows disappear.

"Sometimes fear arises from the understanding of the Lord's all-powerful, all-pervasive, and all-knowing nature. He is the Emperor of the Universe. He is the one who decides and bestows the fruit of all actions. When we think and believe that the Lord is all this, fear and reverence naturally arise. That fear and awe helps us to refrain from committing mistakes. "Arjuna always considered LordKrishna as his close friend, brother-in-law, and expert advisor, and therefore used to address him casually as 'Madhava,' 'Kesava,' and 'Yadava,' which were some of Krishna's different names. But when Arjuna beheld the Lord's universal form, the *Viswarupa*, he was frightened and amazed. In that Viswarupa, Arjuna beheld the entire universe, its beginning, middle and final dissolution. He saw all the gods and goddesses in the Lord's wondrous form. He even saw the Pandava and Kaurava armies existing within the Lord. Arjuna beheld great warriors like Bhisma, Drona, and Karna struggling with death, caught in the Lord's powerful jaws. Now Arjuna saw God as the Supreme Controller and authority, and thus called Him Visweswara, Lord of the Universe.

"Most people want to protect their possessions and their wealth. They believe in God, but they do not want to lose what they have accumulated. They want honor, status and position. In other words, they do not want to give up their egos. Such devotees believe that God can help them to prosper materially. And when they are prosperous, they believe that God will protect their wealth. They have the faith that if God gets angry, He can destroy their wealth and possessions, or that He can snatch everything away. They believe that if God gets angry, He will invoke natural forces like storms, floods, draughts and earthquakes to destroy everything they have. Therefore, they worship God out of fear. They think that they can appease Him through prayer and offerings; and they abstain from things which they think will displease Him. They will perform righteous actions and help others in different ways. They may even build a temple or a church or an orphanage. All this is done to please God, so that they themselves will profit. Nevertheless, this kind of reverence and fear of God is good. At least, it helps people to be good and righteous. Though they do not want to surrender fully to God, and though they don't want to surrender their egos or their attachments, such people are far better than people who don't do any spiritual practices at all.

"A true devotee completelysurrenders to God. He longs for God to kill his ego. That he will not be able to surrender to God or that God won't destroy his ego is a true seeker's greatest fear. Look at the fierce form ofKali. Kali is the destroyer of the ego. Because a true seeker wants to be free from the ego, he will love this aspect of the Divine Mother. Surrendering to Kali or to what she represents, a true devotee will happily offer his head to Her in order to add one more bead to Kali's garland of skulls.

"On the other hand, a devotee who is still attached to possessions and wealth, and to honor and position, will greatly fear this aspect of the Divine. He will never keep a picture of Her in his house or in his puja room. He's afraid that Kali will destroy everything that is dear to him. He thinks that She will kill his ego and that without his ego he cannot exist. An ordinary devotee wants to keep his ego, whereas a true devotee wants to die to his ego so that he can live in consciousness or in pure, innocent love. A true devotee stops feeding the ego; he stops listening to the intellect. He only listens to the heart. Dying to the ego is real death. Thatdeath makes you immortal. Death of the ego leads you to deathlessness. When the ego dies, you live eternally in bliss.

"Amma has heard astory. Once a devotee was about to go to see his spiritual master. Before leaving the house he thought, 'I must offer something to my Guru. Let me take some flowers.' But just as he was about to go, it occurred to him that maybe the flowers were not a good enough offering. So, just in case, he took some diamonds, thinking that if necessary, he could offer these to the Guru as well. The devotee arrived at the place where his master was giving darshan to the public. He went to the master and was about to offer the flowers at his master's feet, when he heard his Guru's voice saying, 'Drop it.' So the devotee dropped the flowers. 'He must want the diamonds,' the devotee thought. But when he tried to offer these, the master again said, "Drop it." Confused, the devotee bent his head and was about to bow to the Guru before getting up to go. But again the master said, 'Drop it.' The puzzled devotee looked up at his master's face. Smiling, the Guru replied, 'Yes, unless you drop your head, the ego, you cannot realize the Self.'"

"Is that what is meant byprostration?" asked a brahmachari.

"Yes," said Mother, "prostration is a symbol of self-surrender. The physical prostration becomes meaningful only when you surrender your ego at the feet of theGuru or God. When you prostrate, you are inviting the Guru or God to trample your ego. The Guru or God will not do that to an ordinary devotee, but they will ruthlessly do it to a true seeker. If you still fear for your security and comfort, if you are still after honor, status and position, the Guru or God will wait. But the day will come when you will renounce all fear for your worldly security and turn fully towards theSatguru or God. Until you realize that you are helpless, that your ego cannot save you, and that all you have acquired is nothing, God or the Guru will keep on creating the circumstances necessary to make you realize this truth. When that happens, you surrender. That is when you cast off all your fear and let the Guru or God dance on your ego while you lie low at His Feet. That is when you become a true devotee. This is the real meaning of prostration.

"The physical prostration that we do now is to lead us to that mental state. Having attained that state, your whole life is a constant prostration to your Guru or Lord. The entire human race, all living beings, the whole of creation is moving towards that state. It does not matter whether or not you resist. It must happen one day, now or later, in this lifetime or the next, your turn will come. Until then you can wait; you can live as you like.

"WhileGod may not be visible to you now, He is always there, guiding and controlling you, holding the reins of your life. To begin with, God allows you long reins, and you don't notice that He is actually in charge. But remember, everything is in God's hands. You are not aware of it, but as you proceed through life, God is gradually shortening the reins. Finally, one day you realize that you cannot move another inch. At that point, when you are utterly helpless, you will feel God tugging at the reins as he begins to pull you back towards Him. You may at first put up a struggle, but you will soon find that the pull is of an unworldly power, and you have no choice but to surrender to His pull. It is at this point that you begin your journey back to God, the Source of your existence. This journey has to happen. You will inevitably find that you can't do anything other than move towards God.

"If God wants to, He can draw in the reins at any time. God thinks, 'This child isn't ready yet. Let him play a little longer. He will tire of it one day. Then he will return.' So be vigilant. Be alert, for you are always under His close watch. You cannot run away from God. Wherever you may go, whatever you may do, He is always there, watching over you, His child. Whatever you do is done only with His consent. He allows you to do it. He lets you play. But you have a limited area to play in. Do not think that you can play anywhere you like.

"At times you may step out of bounds; you may venture where you are not meant to go. It may seem as if God has not noticed, but He is just pretending. God sees and hears everything. At this point He thinks to Himself, 'My child can certainly be mischievous,' and He continues to let you play. But He reminds you that you cannot go on playing forever, by putting you into difficult situations and subjecting you to painful experiences. After a difficult experience you are well-behaved. For a while you remain obedient and calm. But your good behavior is short-lived, and you soon return to your mischievous ways. Now God will think, 'He needs a more painful experience, an even stronger lesson than before.' So God again lets you play a little longer, but He will soon send yet another difficult situation for you to face.

"The lessons learned from this experience have a strong impact on your awareness and cause a great change in you. Each time you are given a painful experience, the effect of the lesson lasts for a longer period of time. But each time, you again wander back into a forbidden playground, and you revert to your old ways. At last God thinks, 'This is too much, I have warned him several times. What he needs now is a real shock.' So God sends a terrible thunderbolt. Once and for all, it puts an end to your play. You crash down helplessly. The thunderbolt hits your ego and breaks it into a hundred pieces.

"For some people, this is a time of revelation. But for others, this becomes a point of total disappointment and frustration. They may lose all interest in life. Their mental agony may be so great that they may commit suicide unless a person endowed with wisdom helps them to see the divine message that is hidden in this excruciating experience. Unless they get proper guidance from a real Master, they are likely to break down completely. Yet, if with the blessings of aSatguru, they are able to open their eyes, they will clearly see the futility of the ego and how it has deluded them. At this point they feel God's pull. They hear His call. They wake up, and for the first time ever they find that they are truly alive. This crashing down of the ego can happen at any time, in this life or the next. It happens sooner for some, while others, because of their lack of maturity, will, with His permission, be allowed to play a little more. At all times, each one of us is being watched over by God. He cannot miss us.

"A spiritualmaster once gave a hen to each of his two disciples and said, 'Take them to a spot where you can kill them without anyone seeing you.' The first disciple walked out and hiding behind a bush, he looked around and made sure that no one was watching. He then killed the hen and brought it right back to his master. The second disciple didn't return until sunset. He was tired and weary, and in his arms he carried the hen, which was still alive. With his head hung low he handed the hen to his master. 'Revered Master,' he said, 'Though I tried and tried, I could not find a single spot where no one would see me; for wherever I went, the hen was always looking at me.' Likewise, children, wherever you go and whatever you do, you are under the watchful eyes of your Guru or God."

At this point Mother asked the brahmacharis to sing a song

Ellam ariyunna (The One who knows everything)

There is no need to tell anything
To the all-knowing Krishna;
He sees and understands everything
As He walks beside us.

The Primordial Being
Sees every thought in the innermost Self;
It is not possible for anyone
To do anything without Him.

The Primordial Lord abides within everyone
We should all worship with joy
That Embodiment of Truth and Awareness.

Chapter 10

Do not compare yourselfwith others

Tuesday, 1 October, 1984

A devotee who had just arrived at the Ashram began explaining to all present how he'd had the darshan of Mother as Krishna. He was very excited as he told the following story: "A week ago I was sleeping in my room when all of a sudden I was awakened by a strong light and an extraordinary fragrance which filled the room. I got up and sat on my bed. The light that permeated the room was as bright as sunlight, yet it was as beautiful and cooling like moonlight. Bathed in this effulgence, my body became so light that I felt I was losing body-consciousness. Suddenly the atmosphere changed. Like water gushing from a dam, peace and supreme bliss filled the air. It was so tangible and penetrating; it engulfed my entire being. The next moment, the divine light that had filled the room seemed to gather together and become concentrated in one particular spot. As I gazed at this concentrated effulgence, the beautiful and enchanting form of LordKrishna emerged."

The devotee could hardly control his excitement. With tears streaming from his eyes, he said, "It was my Lord! But at the same time, it was my Mother also–His face was Mother's face. It was just like Mother in Krishna Bhava–the same smile, the same look, the same eyes–everything was the same. The Lord walked up to me. He had a bowl in His hands. Krishna fed me with butter and *panchamritam*, and He also put some in each of my hands. The Lord gave me a *tulasi* leaf, and then looked into my eyes and placed His right hand on my head. As I looked at His divine form and enchanting smile, the Lord vanished.

"The next morning when I awoke I found myself lying on the floor. I was in what I can only call a semi-conscious mood. Still in bliss, I cried and cried, and found that I was calling out to the Lord and to Mother. It must have taken over two hours before I could function. When I came back to normal consciousness, I tried to recollect everything. But I still couldn't believe this had happened, that the Lord had actually visited me! In order to convince myself, I smelled my hands. And sure enough, they had the smell of butter and the sweet fragrance of panchamritam. It was such a beautiful smell; it remained on my hands for three days. And the taste was in my mouth as well. To my wonderment, I also found a tulasi leaf on my bed. I was in bliss for more than a week, and my heart was full of divine love."

The devotee once again shed tears of love and devotion. Later he went and sat in the darshan hut, where he remained until Mother arrived at eleven o'clock. As She entered the hut, Mother saw the devotee sitting in a corner, deeply absorbed in meditation. As if to let him know that She was aware of all that had happened, Mother exclaimed, "My son!" as She walked up to him and placed Her right hand on his head. The devotee opened his eyes and looked up at Mother, who stood there, gazing at him. There was an extraordinary glow on Her face. With his palms joined, and shedding silent tears of bliss, the devotee gazed back at Her. For a few seconds, no one spoke. But the silence was soon broken when the devotee burst into tears and fell at Mother's feet. After expressing Her love towards him in the form of an affectionate hug, Mother walked over to the cot where She receives Her devotees, and the day's darshan began.

That evening, Mother was sitting in the coconut grove talking with the Ashram residents. One of the householder devotees, who was a good sadhak, mentioned the devotee who'd had the darshan of Krishna and Mother, and said that he was feeling dejected at not having had such a vision.

Mother responded by saying, "Son, don'tcompare yourself with others. This is not good for asadhak. A sadhak should look into himself; he should detect his own mistakes and correct them. You have enough problems of your own to worry about and to work on. Don't make yourself unhappy thinking, 'I will never have an experience like his.' Try to feel happy for him. You should have the attitude that he needed that vision, and that is why Mother or the Lord graciously appeared to him. Think that it was due to his spiritual practices and his strong faith. Don't feel discouraged. Don't think that you are less fortunate than he. What happens with him is meant only for him. And what happens in your life is meant only for you, and has nothing to do with anyone else. Comparison will spoil everything. Whatever happens in your life is the outcome of your ownsamskaras. Your experiences are your own. They cannot be repeated in his or in anybody else's life because each person's samskara is different. What you picked up is different from what he has picked up. And the experiences will differ accordingly. So, there is no sense in comparing and worrying. It will only help to dampen your enthusiasm.

"If you have not been given such an experience, feeling sad about it and calling yourself a sinner or unfit will not help things at all. It will only cause you to close down. It will only destroy any possibility of having such an experience. So give up self-degrading thoughts and strive hard, with determination, for your own vision of the Lord. It must happen if you have the determination and the love.

"Comparison will kill all your talents. Comparison will make you more self-conscious and less efficient. A self-conscious person cannot express himself well. He or she will lose all power of creativity. A person who constantly compares himself with others will constantly think about other people. 'Oh God, why am I not able to sing like him? How I wish I could paint like she does! I should also do tapas like him.' Brooding over what others have, he loses his own power of expression. His talents lie dormant and eventually die. What a fate! A person such as this can never be himself. He will not correct his own mistakes and drawbacks and thus, he can never improve. He is always worried and disgusted with himself. This self-contempt may even make him mentally ill. Never content or happy, he cannot experience the real joy of life.

"Amma remembers a young man who came here once. He had been a good singer with a beautiful, rich voice, and had won the first prize in a university music festival. On the same day that he was awarded the prize, one of his friends had teased him, saying that however much he strove or whatever recognition he got, he could never be as good as the famous film singer, Jesudas. These words wounded him deeply. They hurt him so much that from that day onward he stopped singing and never sang again.

"Upon hearing his friend's words, he thought, 'What he said is true. I can't sing like him. And if I can't sing like Jesudas, then why should I sing at all? It's better not to sing.' This thought, this comparison, struck his mind like lightning. At that moment he must have felt himself to be worthless, and as result, suddenly lost all interest in his singing. He was such a talented singer; he could have become one of the best. But one moment's thought, one fateful comparison, destroyed all possibility for growth.

"So you see, comparison can be very destructive. It will hinder your spiritual progress. It can obstruct all possibilities of mental and intellectual growth. It can cause depression or a serious mental disease. Children, it can affect all aspects of life. Keep in mind that you cannot be someone else and that no one else can be you. You can only be you. Comparison destroys your personality. It will make you look like a fool in front of others. A spiritual seeker should never compare himself or his experiences with someone else's. That is why a sadhak should not disclose his experiences to anyone. Before the attainment of Self-Realization, spiritual experiences can differ. You may never receive a darshan like that son did. And even if you do, it will be different. Some people may feel peace and bliss within, but may never behold the form of a god or goddess. Some may only see an effulgence or a pinpoint of light. It is always different. Different people's experiences cannot be the same. They can only happen according to each individual's unique mental constitution, the path he follows, the amount of effort he puts forth, and the samskaras he has inherited from previous lives. What you experience now is not a beginning; it is a continuation of the past. Also, you must remember that the Guru gives only what is needed, and that whatever he gives is for your own good. The Guru cannot be partial. If you feel upset, thinking that the Guru is partial, that he gives more to others than to you, the problem is within you. We are so judgmental that we cannot see this truth with impartial and discriminating eyes.

"Children, above all else, your innocence and love play a very important role in building up your spiritual life. Receptivity is fundamental to spiritual life. A devotee or disciple should always be receptive."

The child within

"Amma, what do you mean by receptivity? How can one be receptive?" asked a devotee.

"Receptivity comes where there is love within," Mother answered. Love helps you to be open, open like a child. Love makes you innocent like a child. A child is the most receptive person. Receptivity is the power to believe, the power to have faith, the ability to accept love. It is the power to prevent doubt from entering your mind. Receptivity is the ability to accept all experiences of life without reacting to them.

"Receptivity makes you simple. A receptive person is like an innocent child. If you want to be closer to God, try to be like a child. A child's world is full of wonder and imagination and play. As you get older this look of wonder disappears from your eyes. You cannot play anymore. You cannot believe anymore; like so many grown-ups, you can only doubt.

"Have you watchedchildren play? They can imagine that a small sand heap is a big castle. At one moment white sand is sugar for them, and the next moment it is salt. A rope with its ends tied together becomes a car or a bus. For them a rock can be a throne, and a leaf becomes a big fan. Sometimes they imagine that a long coconut frond is a serpent. They can believe in anything. If you tell a child that rain is the water that falls down when the celestial beings who live in the sky wash their dishes, he will believe you; a child won't express any doubt. This openness, the power to accept, is receptivity. Don't think that Amma is asking you to believe in everything people tell you. She is only asking you to have faith in the Satguru's words, and in the words of the great saints and sages who have realized and experienced the ultimate goal of life.

"As we get older, we lose all enthusiasm and joy. We become dry and unhappy. Why? Because we lose our faith and innocence.

It is good for you to spend some time with children. They will teach you to believe, to love and to play. Children will help you smile from your heart and to have that look of wonderment in your eyes.

"There is a child within everyone. The innocence and the playfulness of a child exists in all human beings. People of all ages like children's stories and while hearing or reading them the child within is invoked. Who does not like to play with children now and then? Watch a ninety year-old man, look at a politician or a government administrator, a business executive or a scientist; all will become playful and free when they are around a child. When he is with his grandchildren or his youngest child, even an old man becomes a child. Crawling on all fours, he pretends he is an elephant. He makes a castle out of playing cards for them. Using sticks and leaves, he builds a play house for the little ones. Bouncing the children on his knee, he tells them that he is a horse.

"Why does he do all this? Is it simply to please the child, to make him or her happy? No. That is not the only reason. It is because in each of us a child is hidden. Somewhere in each one of us, a child's joy,innocence, and faith lie dormant. We delight in searching for the child within. When we were children, we had no worries or problems; recalling these days with love, we want to return to them. This desire is felt by all living beings.

"Children, the wonder and the love that you felt as a child will never return unless you can again play like a child. Innocence is within you, hidden deep inside. You have to rediscover it. And for this to happen, you must go deeper and deeper into your spiritual practices. When you can dive deep into your own consciousness, you will realize this innocence one day. At that moment you will discover the child within you. You will experience the innocence, the joy and the wonder that were hidden inside of you, and you will realize they were always there. You merely forgot your innocence for some time. It is as if you suddenly remember something after having forgotten about it for a very long time. That childlike innocence deep within you is God.

"Children, have you heard thisstory? God decided to create the world. His purpose was to give Himself a place to live. So as soon as He had created this beautiful earth full of trees and plants, animals and birds, mountains and valleys, God began to dwell here. Everything was perfect, and God was leading a happy and blissful life. Years rolled by until one day God made a mistake: He created human beings. From that day on, there was trouble. Night and day, the human beings complained to God. No matter what God was doing, whether He was eating or sleeping, they would come knocking on His door.

"The never-ending complaints drove Him crazy. God lost his peace of mind. No sooner was one problem solved than another one arose. The first man's solution became the second man's problem. One person wanted rain, yet when God granted that, another person complained: 'God, how can you do this to me? My whole house is leaking; my crops are all ruined.' Everything became a problem. No matter what God did, people complained.

"Eventually God asked His advisors to suggest a way out. One suggestion was that He go to the Himalayas, but God said, 'No, no. People would soon come there.' 'What about the moon, then?' another of God's advisors asked. 'Soon man would also make his way there.'

'You, my good friends, cannot see the future,' continued God. 'But I can. No matter where I go, man will come to know about it. He will follow Me, and I will again be in trouble.'

"This statement was met with silence. After some time an aged advisor stepped forward and whispered something into God's ear. God's face brightened. 'Wonderful!' He exclaimed.

"The old man had suggested a perfect hiding place for God. 'Go and hide deep within him,' the wise man had advised. 'Yes, it's perfect.' was God's reply. 'Man would never think to look for me inside of him. There is no chance that he will find me there.'

"Children," Mother continued, "God is deep within us. He dwells there asinnocence, as pure and innocent love. Now this innocence is veiled by the mind and its egotistic feelings. But it is always there; it has only been forgotten. You have to go deep within; you have to rediscover and remember.

"Amma, how does thisremembering happen?" asked the same devotee.

"Sometimes when you are trying to remember something, a certain word or a name, you have the feeling that it's on the tip of your tongue. You know that it's there, but still, you can't quite remember it. Pacing back and forth, you think about it. While sitting in your living room, you try to recall the word; and it is still on your mind when you get up to go to your room. But nothing happens and you begin to grow restless. You pull at your hair, you scratch your head, you try and try to remember, but your effort is in vain. After struggling like this for a long time, you finally stop; you give up and soon forget all about the word that you had wanted so much to remember. You even forget all about the effort that you made. Later, having gone outside to relax and to enjoy some solitude, it happens. Suddenly you remember the word. It dawns within you. Only when your efforts ceased, were you able to recall the word. When you work hard during the day, you sleep well at night. Similarly, when you stopped trying to remember, the mind became quiet and still. And in that state of relaxation and stillness the memory could effortlessly emerge.

"Similarly, after doing all yoursadhana, you have to wait for everything to settle down and to sink in. You have to reach a state of complete forgetfulness. When you are lying in bed, you will not make a conscious effort to fall asleep; you will just lie there and wait for sleep to come. You don't think about the past or the future. You just throw yourself in the hands of sleep. You relinquish all control and effortlessly glide into sleep. Likewise, you have to forget about the goal and all the effort you have made to reach it. You must forget about Self-Realization and thespiritual practices you have done to reach that supreme goal. Don't think, 'Oh, what a pity! Even after doing so much sadhana I have not progressed at all.' Such thoughts can also obstruct your way to the final goal. You should neither complain nor think. Thinking will only get in your way; therefore, keep quiet; relax both inside and out. You cannot predict when Grace will happen; you can only wait. It can happen at anytime, at any place. It is up to the Guru or God. It is the Satguru who decides when he should let Grace flow to the disciple. Then, when the time is ripe, all of a sudden it happens: you become a fully conscious, innocent child."

The consciously innocent child

At this time Sreekumar's sister's seven year-old daughter, Takkali, came with her grandparents to see Mother. Though her given name was Sheeja, Mother called her 'Takkali', which means tomato, and so everyone began to call her by that name. Upon seeing the girl, Mother exclaimed, "Oh, you are a grown up girl now. Come here, sit by Amma's side." The girl walked up to Mother and sat down at Her side. Mother lovingly held her hand and kissed the girl on her forehead. Turning to Balu, Mother asked, "Do you know her." Balu said, "Yes, of course I know her, Amma." Holding Takkali tightly, and pointing at Balu, Mother asked, "Do you know him?" "Yes," the girl replied, "that is Baluannan (elder brother Balu)."

Mother then asked her to sing. Closing her eyes, Takkali sang

Orunalil nyan en

Some day I will see Krishna;
I will hear His melodious song
My darling Krishna will come
And stand before me,
With the flute gently pressed
Against His beautiful lips.

On that day, the purpose of my life
Will be fulfilled;
I will be immersed in Bliss,
And on the highest summit of ecstatic devotion,
I will dance in Divine Bliss.

O Sustainer of the Universe,
Are You not the Lord, the Source of all Beings?
O God, let me see You
Without a moment's delay!

When Takkali finished the song, Mother affectionately kissed and hugged her all over again. Obviously delighted, Mother smiled fondly at all who were gathered, praising the little girl's singing and her sweet innocence. As he watched Mother play with young Takkali, one of the brahmacharis was inspired to ask a question, "Amma, you said earlier that one day we will all become conscious, innocent children. How is that possible? What did Amma mean?"

"Children," Mother said, "a small child is not aware of its innocence. His or her innocent nature is completely unconscious. A small child is absolutely pure; he dwells in the state of purity before impurities are manifested. But soon, the child's purity and innocence will begin to disappear. Impurity and ignorance will take their place. The qualities of wonder and joy, imagination and faith, that we see in a child are short-lived. As long as a child remains a child, his innocence is there. But a child changes. Even a child's mind is bound by time and space, therefore time brings about changes even in a child. Thus, the innocent child gradually slips into the clutches of the ego. The unmanifested ego and the accumulated tendencies of past lives gradually manifest, and the child's innocence slowly slips back into an unmanifested state.

"In a grown-up, innocence is dormant, whereas his ego is in full bloom. As the karmic cycle revolves, the time will come for an individual soul to take another birth. When the *jiva* emerges from the womb as a child, the dormant or unmanifested innocence once again manifests, but it will recede again as the ego manifests. This alternating cycle in which the ego manifests and innocence recedes, and vice versa, continues until we turn to God and the ego is eliminated by its root. When the ego is completely eliminated, we become a consciously innocent being; we become eternally innocent. Until that uprooting of the ego takes place, we will have to experience the state of being an unconsciously innocent child through countless lives; that is, we will be born again and again as a child who is not aware or conscious of its innocence.

"While a child's innocence lasts only for a short period of time, a Mahatma is eternallyinnocent. The child has not realized this innocence, whereas the Mahatma has full realization of his innocent and pure nature. One can get a glimpse of God in a child, but the child is not God. A Mahatma is God. A Mahatma lives in Supreme Consciousness. He is beyond the cycle of birth and death. He has the strength and support of his realization. He is wide awake, fully aware and conscious of his realized state. A child is not wakeful to consciousness and has no realization of its pure nature. It is still fast asleep to that state. This is a vast difference, isn't it? The Self-Realized state of the Mahatma is what Amma meant by conscious innocence."

Mother's words having penetrated deep into their hearts and minds, everyone sat quietly for some time after She had finished speaking. Glancing briefly at each person, Mother's gaze finally rested on Br. Pai and She asked him to sing

Kattutta Sokamam

Let me not fall into this dark pit of sorrow
I am neither a scholar,
Nor was I born under a lucky star.
O Mother, though You know all this,
Don't simply smile at me and walk away
When my thoughts are intensely fixed on You.

O Embodiment of Compassion,
Remove my ignorance,
And bestow pure intelligence on me.
Though in the midst of worldly pleasures,
I am never happy;
I am always gazing at You.
O Ruler of all the worlds,
Giver of true greatness,
Light the lamp of equal vision
Within my innermost Self.

O Mother,
The hummingbird of my mind
Has flown to Your Lotus Feet;
To prevent it from flying away,
Please close Your petals and enfold it.
O greater than the greatest,
Let me dive deep within
And enjoy Your nectar of Bliss.

O Quintessence of the four Vedas,
I bow to You.

Your stream of Love flows towards me
In the form of anger;
Your terrifying laughter
Is like a gentle smile to me.
Understanding the unreal nature
Of this dream-like world,
I have taken leave of it
I will never be separated from You,
Who have showered Your nectarine Grace upon me.

Forgiving and forgetting

Wednesday, 2 October, 1984

During this morning's darshan a devotee began complaining to Mother about her husband. She described at great length how uncooperative and loveless he was. She said that she felt like leaving him because of the unbearable situation.

Wiping away the woman's tears, Mother replied, "Daughter, problematic situations are difficult to avoid. You are not the only one with such problems. Everywhere in the world, people are suffering like you. If you try to run away from this situation, another difficult situation will await you; no matter where you go or what you choose to do with your life, problems will arise. It could be worse than this, you know. You'll never feel peaceful or happy if you don't have patience and humility. Family life will be miserable as long as the family members lack these virtues. Nowadays it is difficult to find a family where both the husband and the wife are patient; but one of them, either the husband or the wife, should exercisepatience. In most cases both are 'patients without patience', but unless there is a balance, unless a certain amount of patience is exercised on both sides, a harmonious family life will be impossible.

"There is a tendency in human beings to run away from difficult situations. You think that running away will save you or help rid you of your sorrows. You might even change to another situation which you hope will be more comfortable. Initially you may feel wonderful and peaceful after making such a change. You don't realize that you are only running towards yet another problem. If you go to live with your parents, relatives or friends, when you first arrive, you might be given a warm welcome. They will express great sympathy and love for you in all that they say and do. They will all embrace you and cry; you will exchange promises, and wet each other's shoulders with tears.

"But within a few days, or in a week or two at the most, the situation will change. This will happen because when you ran away from the previous situation you did not leave your ego. It followed you. You carried it with you, and along with it, all your impatience and lack of humility. So after a short while in this new place, negativity starts to manifest. You begin to find fault with someone in the family, or the situation you are in. You grow impatient with your mother or your father, your brother or sister, or your friend, and they begin to react, because they, too, have their own vasanas. They cannot bear your impatience or disobedience. Soon you will realize that you have run from one problem right into another, and that this new situation might even be worse than the one you left. When you were together with your husband, he at least didn't kick you out of the house. After an argument, he used to repent and there was always a reconciliation. But now your friends or relatives may ask you to leave. And the only thing gained from all this is more resentment, more frustration, and more negative feelings.

223

"Daughter, whether you are living all alone or with a family, your life will not be happy and successful unless you have the mental capacity to adapt to any situation. This is one of life's most basic principles. You may think that living alone is the way to be happy, but you will have problems even then. As long as you are gripped by prejudices and preconceived ideas, you cannot be free from the difficulties of life.

"However, getting rid of the ego is not an easy thing to do. Daughter, you think that your husband is uncooperative and that he doesn't love you. But there must have been times when he was loving and cooperative. Amma can't believe that he is always so bad. If he's as bad as you say he is, he must be a monster."

Mother stopped for a while and looked at the woman's face. She replied, "No, of course he's not. Sometimes he is very loving and sweet."

Smiling, Mother once again questioned the woman, "How did you feel when he was loving and sweet?" The woman blushed and said, "I felt comfortable and happy. I was also loving to him." "And when he was unfeeling and difficult?" Mother inquired. "I felt terribly angry and closed," responded the woman.

Smiling mischievously, Mother continued, "Daughter, these reactions and feelings are common. Human beings naturally have such feelings towards each other. Still, you should try to respect and admire your husband's good qualities. When he shows you no love or when he is not cooperative, you react, don't you? And haven't there been times when it was you who started the fight with him?" The woman hung her head. She had nothing to say.

Mother continued, "So, you do react to him. Don't worry, it's all right. But, at that moment, instead of reacting, try to listen patiently, try to remain calm. Later, when he is in a good mood, when you get an opportunity, you can talk to him in a very loving way. Then he will listen and understand because his mind is calm. Don't throw your ideas at him when he is angry. He won't listen then. Learn to keep quiet at that time; don't listen to your ego then. When he has left the house, you should go and sit either in your family shrine room or in a solitary place where you can contemplate and think deeply.

"While sitting there, try to recall the whole incident. Try to remember how the scene began. If it started when you insisted that he do something, and he refused; now you should try to remember a time when he bought something for you or did you a favor as soon as you asked. Remember how nice he was at that time. Think of another occasion when he was patient and forgiving, even when you yourself were impatient and rude. Try to recall the sleepless nights he spent sitting beside you when you were hospitalized. Try to appreciate the loving care and consoling words which helped you so much at the time. He had to work the whole day, yet he took a lot of time and trouble to make you feel happy and comfortable. Think of a few occasions when he tried to make up with you after you'd quarreled over a silly matter. Also, you should try to remember how angry and impatient you were throughout the incident, and how impolitely you spoke to him.

"Contemplating these memories will surely help you to feel better about the situation. These moments of solitude will enable you to see the incident with more clarity and understanding. You may even begin to feel remorse for your own harsh and impatient behavior. By the time your husband comes home in the evening, you will have prepared yourself to face him, and will be able to receive him with a big smile. You offer him a good cup of coffee. While he sips the coffee, you first of all apologize for your behavior in the morning, then you ask him whether the headache he had in the morning was still there or gone. Suppose he says, 'No, it is still there.' You take some balm and rub it on his forehead, then you lovingly inquire about the day's happenings at the office. You try to console him about his boss being rude to him on that day.

"Your husband will look at you in wonder, 'Is this the same wife whom I fought with this morning?' Even if he has harbored some anger or resentment, it will melt. His attitude will change. Filled with remorse, he spontaneously apologizes for his rude behavior. Now is your opportunity to explain to him whatever you want. You tell him everything and he listens with great interest. He then tells you whatever he wants to say and you pay great attention to that. Thus, what began as an argument evolves into a great event. It becomes an opportunity for reconciliation and sharing. You are full of love for one another. Both of you feel happy and relaxed.

"Married life is not a joke. It is something that should be taken seriously.Relationships can become a path to God, a path to eternal freedom and peace, provided you have the right attitude. Don't automatically consider separation each time you feel uncomfortable. Strive to be adaptable. Try to be patient, not once or twice, but many times.

"Man is extremely impatient, but God is immenselypatient and careful about His creation. Impatience destroys. Think of the warning you see on road signs, 'Speed kills.' Speeding is impatience. Human beings are impatient; they are always in a hurry. Hurrying is necessary sometimes. But mostly, hurrying kills. When you give medicine to someone who is critically ill, don't hurry. Even if the medicine must be given immediately, even if it is an emergency case, still you should not hurry. If you hurry, in your excitement, your hands might tremble while pouring water into the patient's mouth while giving him pills to swallow. You may miss and water might go into the nose. That can cause trouble. In your hurry, you may give too much or even the wrong medicine to the patient, and this could kill him. Be patient. Real life is love. When you love, you cannot hurry. You must be patient.

"Look at the care and patience God showers on His creation. A tiny flower may not last for more than a day. But still, God is very careful and patient with it, providing it with water and sun until it finally blossoms. The hatching of an egg and the birth of a child require great care and patience. It takes nine long months of nurturing before a child is born. God is not at all in a hurry.

"Think of the suffering your mother endured when you were in her womb for nine long months. She carried you with no complaints, and happily endured all discomfort and pain. She could do this because she knew that all pain would disappear when she saw you, when she saw her baby's beautiful face. Daughter, in this way, you should bear with your pain by thinking of the peaceful and harmonious life which you will have if you are able to endure. It doesn't matter who is at fault. Sometimes it will be your husband, and at other times, it will be you. But whoever is to blame, just try to do what Amma has said, and see what happens."

"Practice forgiveness. If there are still difficulties in a relationship even after you put forth a lot of effort, you can consider it your karma, your destiny. At this point you can either endure it, accepting the difficulties as your *prarabdha;* or, if you find the situation too difficult to withstand anymore, maybe you can think of separation or divorce. But before that, you must play your part well. You must put forth effort at least to see whether the relationship can work or not. To simply let it fall apart is an unpardonable mistake. It is a sin and you will have to suffer for it."

Full of compassion, Mother looked at the woman's face. She was again crying, but this time they were tears of repentance. She had realized her mistake. Through her tears, the woman asked Mother to forgive her for her faults. Her voice was full of remorse as she continued to speak. "Now I understand that I am also to blame, and not just today but always. I, too, am responsible for our conflicts. I was the one who triggered them. Had I kept quiet and acted as you advised, this situation would not have happened. However, Amma you have opened my eyes. From now on I will try my best to control myself and to keep quiet on such occasions. I will try to act just as Amma has instructed."

Daughter," Mother said, "whenever such a situation arises, if you can pause and bepatient, your problems can easily be solved. But it is our habit to react. When anger arises, we cannot pause and see clearly; we cannot wait. When you are in the midst of an upsetting situation, can you simply observe what is happening? Can you stop thinking that someone is insulting and abusing you? Can you forget that you are being treated unfairly and let go of the wish to do something about it? Don't be abusive. Don't react. Try to realize that the real problem is not what is happening, but how you are reacting to it. When you see that you are going to react negatively, at this point, pause. Stop talking. Say to your mind, 'No, don't say anything now. You will get a better opportunity to present the whole matter in a more effective way. But now you keep quiet for the time being.'

"During this pause, try to think of something positive, something elevating, something sweet, something that you consider unforgettable. Try to recall a pleasant event or memory. Focus all your energies, all your thoughts on that. If you can do this, you won't be bothered or angered by the ridiculous words and unbearable face of the other person.

"If you can, try to make this pause last longer and longer. Whenever you find that you are feeling even a little bit angry or annoyed, you can experiment. To begin with, you can choose some silly matter to which you are used to reacting. For example, say your husband has a habit of tapping his fingers on the table whenever he is lost in thought, and you find the sound irritating.

Instead of saying anything, think of the sound as coming from raindrops falling on the roof. You might then remember a time when you and your husband got caught in the rain and together you ran for shelter under a tin awning. Rather than getting angry or annoyed, let your imagination and associations put you in a positive, even a loving mood.

"In due course, when you have learned to overcome these mildly provoking situations, you can slowly begin to test your experiment in more trying and serious situations. As you continue to practice, you will see that you are changing. And eventually, you will see that you cannot react anymore, that you can only respond. You will experience much more peace and joy in your marriage and in your family life in general. The change in your attitude and the patience that you show will also create a positive change in others.

"When your husband sees that you are not reacting any-more, when he realizes that his anger and insults are no longer being accepted, that they are no longer affecting you, he will feel embarrassed. What happens when a warrior finds that his weapons are not powerful or effective anymore? He throws them away. Similarly, when your husband finds that his weapons, the words that he uses against you, are not hurting you anymore, he will give up and keep quiet. In addition, you will now be treating him with more love and care. This is a great gift. Your smiling face and loving inquiries, your care and comforting words will serve as a balm, as a great relief and consolation to him. He will forget everything, all his anger, failures and any resentment that he has harbored. If he was working hard the whole day, if he was scolded by his boss and comes home with his head full of troubles, and you can give that gift to him, or to her (it does not matter whether it is the husband or the wife who shows this attitude), he or she will become your best friend and admirer. Great love and concern will develop in the relationship. Therefore daughter, before getting upset, pause, wait and be patient.

"Amma will tell you astory. There was a professor who had been invited to deliver a speech. He did not prepare the speech well and, as a result, his talk was not very good. A few days later, he received a letter from one of the listeners. The content of the letter was as follows, 'Dear sir, if you are not very knowledgeable, you would be wise not to speak, rather than give false ideas and create a bad impression on your audience.' The signature on the letter was a woman's.

"Upon reading the letter, the professor was furious. He immediately sat down at his typewriter and pounded out a fiery and burning response to his critic, full of the choicest harsh words. As soon as he was finished, he went to post it, but he realized then that the day's mail had already gone. So he put the letter aside. The next morning when he saw the letter on his desk, he thought, ' Maybe I wasn't polite enough to this person. Let me go through the letter once again before I mail it.' So he opened the letter and read it, and was shocked to see how rudely he had reacted. He said to himself, 'This is certainly not a very polite letter. I should definitely not mail it in its present form.' So he sat down and drafted another letter which, though milder in its expressions and images, was still abusive.

"He was about to mail this second letter when he thought, 'Wait a minute, let me read it one more time. Maybe the tone is still not right. If my attitude could change so much in just a few hours, maybe it can still change.' So he read the letter again and finding the tone still too harsh, he rewrote it. But still he did not feel good about the letter, so he changed and rewrote it a few more times until finally, it became a love letter. In it, the professor confessed his mistakes and agreed with the woman; he even mentioned how gracious it was of her to point out his drawbacks.

'People like you are really helpful. I am very grateful to you,' he wrote. 'If you are not married, I would like to ask you to be my wife. Eagerly awaiting your positive reply, I am yours truly.'

"The poison that the professor was at first emitting was transformed into nectar. Sometimes you may make a bad decision, or judge someone wrongly, or you may act in an indiscriminate way. But, if you can pause, wait patiently, and contemplate the matter, you will not run into trouble. This is what you gain from patience and proper contemplation. Therefore, daughter, be patient and contemplate matters well before you act. Amma is with you. Don't worry."

At this point the woman fell into Mother's lap. "Amma, forgive me for my mistakes!" she cried. "Forgive me! I will try not to repeat them again. Forgive me." Expressing Her love and compassion to the woman, Mother consoled her and helped her to relax. Before she left the Ashram a short while later, the woman seemed to be fully at peace. She wore a big smile on her face, a clear sign that her sorrows had been unburdened.

In the *Lalita Sahasranama*, Devi is praised as *Tapa-trayagni-samtapta-samah-ladana-chandrika*, which means 'the moonlight that gladdens the hearts of those who are tormented by the fire of misery.' This misery, it is explained, is caused by the sense organs, both internal and external, by the objective world which they mediate, and by supernatural powers beyond the visible world. This mantra is equally applicable to a Great Soul like Mother, who is Devi or the Divine Mother incarnate. Through Her compassionate and soothing looks, Her profound words and divine touch, or by Her presence alone, Mother bestows this blessing of healing human hearts. Only a Realized Master, one who has attained the state Perfection can save human beings from this triple misery. Such a being alone can give repose and solace to people afflicted by the sufferings incidental to birth, old age and dying.

Glossary

Certain words are the same or similar in Malayalam and Sanskrit. Thus *Abhyasa* and *Brahmachari* are Sanskrit whereas *Abhyasam* and *Brahmacharin* are Malayalam

Adharma: Unrighteousness, sin, opposed to Divine Harmony

Agamas: Scriptures

Ammachi: The Mother. *Chi* is a word indicating respect.

Anooraniyaan Mahatomahiyan: Sanskrit for "Subtler than the subtlest, bigger than the biggest," a description of Brahman, the Supreme Reality.

Arati: Waving the burning camphor, which leaves no residue, with ringing of bells at the end of *puja* (worship) indicating total annihilation of ego.

Archana: A mode of worship by repetition of one hundred, three hundred or a thousand names of the deity.

Arjuna: The third among the Pandavas and a great archer.

Ashram: Hermitage or residence of a sage.

Atma(n): The Self

Atma bodha: Self-knowledge or Self-awareness

Avadhut(a): A Realized Soul who has transcended all social conventions.

Bhagavad Gita: The teachings of Lord Krishna to Arjuna at the beginning of the Mahabharata War. It is a practical guide for common man for every day life and is the essence of Vedic wisdom. *Bhagavad* means 'that of the Lord' and *Gita* means 'Song', particularly, an advice.

Bhagavata(m): The book about the Incarnations of Lord Vishnu, especially Krishna and His childhood antics. It upholds the supremacy of devotion.

Bhagavati: The Goddess of six virtues, viz, prosperity, valor, auspiciousness, knowledge, dispassion and lordship.

Bhajan: Devotional singing
Bhakti: Devotion.
Bhava: Mood.
Bhava Darshan: The occasion when Amma receives devotees in the exalted state of the Universal Mother.
Bhoga: Enjoyment
Bhrantan: Having the nature of a madman, alluding to the nature or appearance of some Realized Souls.
Brahman: The Absolute, Whole.
Brahmachari: A celibate student under training of a Guru.
Brahmacharya: Celibacy
Dakshina: Reverential offering in cash or kind.
Darshan: Audience of a Holy Person or deity.
Deva: Demi-god, celestial being
Devi: The Goddess.
Devi Bhava: Divine Mood of, or identity with, the Goddess
Devi Mahatmyam: A sacred hymn in praise of the Goddess.
Dharma: Righteousness, in accordance with Divine Har-mony.
Dhritharasthra: Blind king and father of the Kauravas.
Duryodhana: Eldest son of Dhritharasthra, villain of the Mahab-harata War.
Gita: Song, See *Bhagavad Gita*
Gopas: Cowherd boys, companions of Sri Krishna.
Gopis: Cowherd girls, known for their supreme devotion to Sri Krishna.
Guru: Spiritual Master / Guide.
Guru Paduka Stotram: Hymn of five verses to the Guru's Sandals.
Jagat: The ever-changing world.
Japa: Repetition of a mystical formula (*mantra*)
Jñana: Spiritual or divine wisdom
Kamsa: Lord Krishna's demonic uncle whom He killed.
Kanji: Rice porridge.

Kanna: Name for Krishna.

Karma: Action.

Kauravas: The hundred children of Dhritarashtra, enemies of the Pandavas, who fought in the Mahabharata War.

Kindi: Fluted metallic water pot usually used in worship.

Kirtan: Hymns

Krishna: Principle Incarnation of Lord Vishnu

Lakshmana: Brother of Lord Rama.

Lakshmi: Consort of Lord Vishnu and Goddess of wealth.

Lakshya Bodha: Constant awareness of and intent on the goal.

Lalita Sahasranama: Thousand names of the Universal Mother in the form of *Lalitambika*

Leela: Divine play.

Mahabharata(m): Great epic written by Vyasa.

Mahatma: Great Soul

Mantra: Sacred formula, the repetition of which can awaken one's spiritual energies and bring the desired results.

Maya: Illusion.

Mol: Daughter. *Mole* is the vocative form.

Mon: Son. *Mone* is the vocative form

Mudra: A sign by hand indicating mystic spiritual truths.

Mukta: The Liberated One

Mukti: Liberation.

Namah Shivaya: The Panchakshara Mantra (mantra consisting of five letters) meaning "Salutations to the Auspicious One (Shiva)."

Om: Mystical syllable representing the Supreme Reality.

Pada puja: Worship of the Guru's feet or sandals.

Pandavas: The five children of King Pandu and heroes of the epic *Mahabharata*

Prarabdha: Responsibilities or burdens. Also, the fruits of past actions manifesting as the present life.

Prasad: Consecrated offerings distributed after *puja*.

Prema: Deep Love.

Puja: Worship.

Rama: Hero of the epic *Ramayana*. An incarnation of Vishnu and the ideal of Righteousness.

Ravana: The villain of the *Ramayana*

Rishi: A great sage or seer.

Sad-asad-rupa dharini: One who dons the form of existence and non-existence, a name of the Divine Mother.

Sadhak: One dedicated to attaining the spiritual goal, one who practices *sadhana* (spiritual discipline).

Sadhana: Spiritual practices.

Sahasranama: Hymns consisting of the Thousand Names of God.

Samadhi: State of absorption in the Self.

Samsara: The world of plurality, the cycle of birth and death.

Samskaras: Mental tendencies accumulated from past actions.

Sankalpa: Creative, integral resolve manifesting as thought, feeling and action. The sankalpa of an ordinary person does not always bear corresponding fruit. The sankalpa of a sage, however, always bears the intended result.

Sannyasi(n): Ascetic who has renounced all worldly bondages.

Satguru: Realized Spiritual Master.

Satsang: Company of the wise and virtuous. Also, a spiritual discourse by a sage or scholar.

Shakti: The dynamic aspect of *Brahman* as the Universal Mother.

Shiva: The static aspect of *Brahman* as the male principle.

Sishya: Disciple.

Sita: Wife of Rama.

Sloka: Sanskrit verse.

Sraddha: Faith. Amma uses it with a special emphasis on alertness coupled with loving care of the work in hand.

Sri Rama: See *Rama*. *Sree, or Sri,* is a mark of respect

Srimad Bhagavatam: see *Bhagavatam*. *Srimad* means 'auspicious'

Stenah: Thief.

Sutra: Aphorism.

Tablas: A type of Indian drum.

Tampura: Stringed instrument which gives a droning sound, the underlying "sruti" of Indian music.

Tapas: Literally "heat." The practice of spiritual austerities.

Tapasvi: One engaged in penance or spiritual austerities.

Tapovan: Hermitage, a place conducive to meditation and tapas.

Tattva: Principle.

Tulasi: The sacred basil plant worshipped as a goddess.

Upanishads: The concluding portion of the Vedas dealing with the philosophy of Non-dualism.

Vasana: Latent tendency.

Veda: Lit. 'Knowledge', the authoritative Scriptures of the Hindus.

Veda Vyasa: See *Vyasa*.

Vedanta(m): The philosophy of the Upanishads which declare the Ultimate Truth as 'One without a Second.'

Vedantin: A follower of the Vedanta philosophy.

Vedic Dharma: Injunctions on the righteous way of living as prescribed by the Vedas.

Vidyavidya svarupini: Whose nature is knowledge and ignorance, a name of the Divine Mother.

Vishnu: All-pervading. The Lord of sustenance.

Vishwarupa: The Universal Form of God.

Vishweshwara: Lord of the Universe.

Viveka: Discrimination.

Vyasa: A sage who divided the one *Veda* into four and composed 18 *Puranas* and also the *Mahabharata* and *Bhagavatam*. As he divided the one *Veda* into four, he is also known by the name of *Veda Vyasa*.

www.ingramcontent.com/pod-product-compliance
Lightning Source LLC
LaVergne TN
LVHW051549080426

835510LV00020B/2916